March,

TO Louise,

May This book help

To understand This

crazy county of ours,

and may we

Keep The Faith.

Love
+
blessings,
Steffon

The Astrological Karma of the USA

By
Steffan G. Vanel

Spiritual Company Press

The Astrological Karma of the U.S.A.

First Edition published in 2002 as:
The United States of America
A Celestial View

Published by:
Spiritual Company Press
P.O. Box 476
Curlew, WA 99118

ISBN 0-9719330-6-5

Printed in the United States of America

Towards a Vision
of a
Truly Beautiful
America

TABLE OF CONTENTS

SUPPLEMENTAL CHAPTERS TO THE SECOND EDITION

FOREWORD TO THE 2ND EDITION

"The teacher appears when the student is ready." Such was the case on a cold January night in 1993, when I met Steffan Vanel for the first time. I responded to a newspaper ad -- something I almost never do -- concerning a lecture he was giving in Atlanta on the Kabbalistic approach to the Tarot. Frankly, I was in over my head, as I didn't even know what "Kabbalistic" meant, let alone how to spell the word. And up until that point, I think the only time I had seen a Tarot deck was in a James Bond film. Nevertheless, I felt compelled to attend.

Thinking back, I was struck by Steffan's low-keyed demeanor, which was in sharp contrast to his thin frame and crisp features. Moreover, there was an underlying wisdom in his voice, a knowingness. It was almost as if he emanated from another place, another time, maybe another world. I impulsively booked a private reading with him two days later. It turned out to be a prophetic, snowy Sunday morning that changed my life. Figuratively speaking, Steffan "took me to church." He offered a glimpse of myself I hadn't seen before. At the risk of sounding cliché, it was both exciting and scary at the same time. I guess you could say I was reborn during the winter of my discontent.

More than 10 years and countless readings later, Steffan continues to play a major role in my life. He is not only a gifted Astrologer, but also my spiritual advisor. My teacher. My friend. His insight has navigated me through many of life's winding roads, including difficult relationships and rocky career changes. Most importantly, Steffan has been a guiding force in my marriage. The fact I've been happily wedded for five years and have a two-year-old daughter is a testament to his good counsel. No wonder my wife, who's known Steffan almost as long as I, considers him family. When embarking on a difficult decision, we think of his insight as a kind of Astrological AmEx card: "We don't leave home without it."

Much of Steffan's popularity rests in the fact he is in the world but not of it. A product of the Sixties counterculture movement, he has since circled the globe relentlessly, studying, sharing, and honing his gifts. Steffan's deep understanding of and compassion for all peoples has allowed him to amass a diverse international clientele. At the heart of his work is a two-fold approach to Astrological interpretation -- Jungian psychological thought coupled with channeled insights from the Ascended Master Hilarion -- that seems to speak to multiple generations, be they Baby Boomers or Gen-Xers.

This delicate interplay between science and metaphysics has a strong spiritual component. Steffan will be the first to admit he's not a psychic, at least, not in the popular sense. He's a guide, motivated not by profit or instilling fear, but by a sense of compassion and unconditional love. What separates Steffan from many Astrologers is that he prefers to not predict the future. Instead, he uses one's birthchart to look at the big picture: the general lessons and experiences one has agreed to take on during this lifetime. Like Hilarion, Steffan believes the only good prophet is a false prophet, one whose warnings have so impressed his/her listeners that they alter their lives for the better, thus averting what has been foreseen.

Hence, this book is not as much about specific prophecies as it is about the big picture. It was originally inspired by a lecture given Sept. 12, 2001, in Eugene, Oregon, for which Steffan, at the last minute, created an Astrological birthchart for the United States. The purpose of it was to examine the significance of the previous day's events through the language of Astrology. Just as an Astrologer can compose a birthchart for a person, he/she can do the same for any entity, such as a business or nation. For the next six months, Steffan launched into a deep exploration of the soul and psyche of the United States, resulting in the first edition of this book.

Steffan has since spent the better part of the last two years working on this second edition. In addition to improving the layout and design, he has added new chapters about President Bush and presidential candidate John Kerry, the end of the Mayan Calendar, conspiracy theory, and the purpose of existence. The result is what you see here: a compelling statement, exploring the lessons, challenges, and possible destiny of one of the greatest nations in the world.

Drawing mainly on the U.S. birthchart, Steffan opens the book by examining 9/11, which he refers to as a "Plutonian wake-up call." He pinpoints, with scientific clarity, how a series of transits in 2000 between Pluto (the bringer of change) and affecting the U.S.' Sagittarian Ascendant (governing self-image and personality), not only triggered Bush's rise to power, but also set the stage for a "fated uncertainty." The real question following 9/11, he asks, is whether the United States will be stirred into the "right kind" of action or allow itself to be lulled back to ignorance and disillusionment. The answer lies not as much in the heavens, but in Americans' willingness to work with, not against, Pluto's beneficial energies.

From there, Steffan turns the clock back some 225 years and plunges into an in-depth analysis of American history. Considerable attention is paid to what he labels the three sources of U.S. Astrological tension: the Saturn/Jupiter square, personified by an ongoing resentment of authority, played out in such events as the Revolutionary and Civil wars; the Pluto/Mercury opposition, whose tension has resulted in much "fuzzy thinking" about sexuality, wealth, and money, spurring everything from slavery and the Great Depression to heated debate over AIDS, homosexuality, and abortion; and the Mars/Neptune square, whose victim/victimizer and "first-we-hate-them-then-we-love-them" themes persist in everything from McCarthyism and the Cold War to the ongoing conflicts in the Middle East. In particular, Pluto's opposition to Mars and square to Neptune between now and 2006 will be a time of great tests and trials, not unlike what occurred in the Sixties.

As Steffan explains, the main purpose of Astrology is to investigate the various relationships, or tensions, between planets in a birthchart and explain their influences. This kind of information, while seemingly negative and disturbing, yields tremendous power and responsibility. Only when these tensions are healed and integrated within one's self or one's nation does true growth occur. It's this dynamism and drama, he writes, that forces people to grow and, ultimately, operate from a higher perspective.

Fortunately, the world is blessed with angels like Steffan to help lead the way.

Rob Enslin
Nazareth College
Rochester, NY

THE ASTROLOGICAL BIRTHCHART OF
THE UNITED STATES OF AMERICA

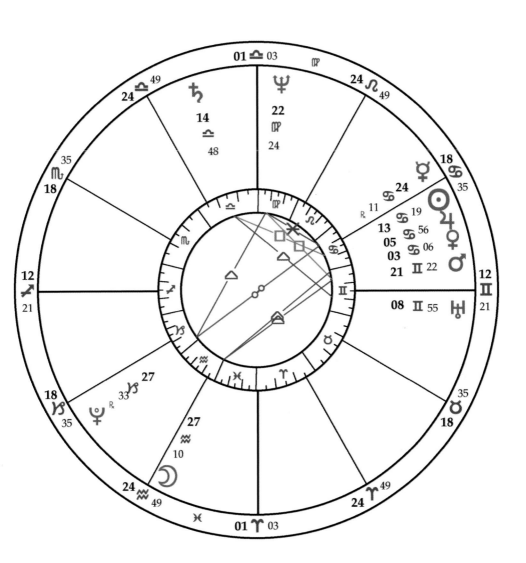

United States of America
Natal Chart
Saturday, July 4, 1776
5:10:00 PM LMT
Philadelphia, Pennsylvania
Tropical   Porphyry   True Node

PREFACE

911. The number to call when you have an emergency. Probably the intended message of the organizers of the terror which struck in New York and Washington on the 11th day of the 9th month of September in 2001. Or perhaps, it was a more curious twist of fate which seared those symbolic numbers into our national psyche on that day. Either way, the violence of September 11th resulted in the most casualties on American soil since Pearl Harbor, the most within the continental U.S. since our Civil War, and the most within the Northeastern U.S. since the Revolutionary War. The scale and shock of this violence has sent a call of emergent alarm throughout our nation and throughout the world.

In August of 2001 I had arranged to give an Astrology lecture in Eugene, Oregon on the evening of September 12. In light of the preceding day's events I quickly changed the topic of my lecture. To that end I calculated the Astrological Birthchart for the United States of America. Astrologers routinely create a map of the heavens calculated for the birthdate, time and place of an individual so as to provide insight into the character, lessons and possible destiny of that individual. What is less commonly known is that a birthchart can be calculated for any entity with a known specific birthdate, time and place, whether that entity be a marriage, a corporation or a nation.

There are various birthdates, times and places used by Astrologers to calculate the birthchart of the United States. Most Astrologers now concur that the events of September 11 have validated the accuracy of the Sibley birthchart. This chart is based upon an engraving entitled Revolution of America found in Ebenezer Sibley's *New and Complete Illustration of the Occult Sciences*, originally published in 1787. It shows the infant United States inscribing the Declaration of Independence. Looking on are a Native American Indian and a British Military officer. In the background there stands the Goddess of Justice with her balancing scales. An angel blowing a trumpet holds an Astrological chart entitled American Independence. This chart was calculated for the local time and latitude of London, England. When the chart is relocated to the local time and latitude of Philadelphia, Pennsylvania, we obtain the chart which many Astrologers have used for the U.S., including Dane Rudhyar, one of the founding fathers of Modern Astrology.

I am sure that on September 12 many of us Astrologers were looking intently to find clues to the symbolic meaning of the September 11 events. I had never studied the Astrological chart for the U.S. before that day. In looking at the Sibley chart for some significance to that horrible violence, I was quite amazed to see not only Pluto the planet of complete transformation, bearing upon the exact degree of the Zodiac representing the self-image of the United States at the time of the bombing, but to also see the full symbolic map of the American character, lessons and our possible destiny.

Since that September 12 lecture I decided to take the Astrological insights I have obtained regarding our nation's identity and the Astrological influences coming to bear upon that identity, now and in the near future, and embody those insights into a book.

In my lecture that evening I made the following statement: "When I find myself in a situation where somebody is confronting me with a powerful or aggressive oppositional energy, and I can see that their behavior is coming from an irrational motivational place, I try to go inside myself and say OK God, I see where this person is coming from. But nonetheless, why is this happening to me? What is the lesson for me in this?" The ability to step back and ask God this question obviously comes from a spiritual faith and trust that everything happens for a reason, that there is always some lesson to be learned, for all parties involved.

It is in that spirit that I write this book to hopefully, help my own country to better understand itself and the lessons coming to bear upon it now, and in the future. I hope that this book can also serve as an aid to life and consciousness in the other nations we share this planet with as well, and to whatever ultimate role and position this planet is to play in the grander scheme of all created things.

Sincerely,
Steffan G. Vanel
January 21, 2002
Martin Luther King Day

INTRODUCTION

Although this book will present an Astrological view of the United States, my hope is that the information presented here may reach a wider public than simply those interested in studying the science of Astrology. To that end I intend to explain the information in the same manner in which I would explain a Birthchart to a client who has a limited knowledge of Astrological symbolism. This will necessarily entail some brief lessons in 'Astrologese' as it were. At the same time, I have included information which is not commonly known in the Astrological community at this time. It is this information which will be of particular interest to the more experienced Astrologer.

My practice as an Astrologer incorporates two schools of Astrological interpretation. One is a psychological approach, popularized by several modern Astrologers. The distinguished Swiss psychologist Carl Gustav Jung expressed his appreciation of Astrology in a 1947 letter to the editor of The Astrological Magazine:

> Since you want to know my opinion about astrology I can tell you that I've been interested in this particular activity of the human mind since more than 30 years. As a psychologist I am chiefly interested in the particular light the horoscope sheds on certain complications in the character. In cases of difficult psychological diagnosis I usually get a horoscope in order to have a further point of view from an entirely different angle. I must say that I very often found that the astrological data elucidated certain points which I otherwise would have been unable to understand.[1]

I combine this psychological approach with Astrological insights derived from a source known as Hilarion. Recognized in various metaphysical schools as an Ascended Master, Hilarion is an advanced human soul presently existing on a non-physical plane of being.[2] Hilarion's approach to Astrology uses the Birthchart to view the lessons, experiences, and potentials which the individual soul has agreed to work on and grow through in this lifetime.

Obviously, applying this information to a nation rather than an individual is quite a different enterprise. However, if one accepts the notion that each individual nation bears its own unique identity, character and destiny, then virtually the same principles can be applied to a nation as to an individual. Indeed, this allegiance to a national identity is something which individuals often use in creating their individual beliefs and actions. A classic example is our own nation's concept of 'manifest destiny,' the belief in the 1800's that it was God's will that our nation should expand its territorial boundaries to encompass the North American continent, from the Atlantic to the Pacific shorelines. The possibility that we would, for various reasons, collectively identify with such a belief can be seen in our Astrological make-up.

The Master Hilarion, one of the main sources of my Astrological knowledge, has dictated through the mediumship of Maurice Cooke a book entitled 'Nations.' This book contains commentaries on the personal lessons and possible destinies of twenty-five different countries in the world.

In the Epilogue to this book Hilarion states:

This booklet has been transmitted for several purposes. The first is to allow an overview of events on the earth plane which is more spiritually oriented than viewpoints typically expressed by man. The second is to offer to incarnated souls certain lessons in the form of allegories, based on the experience of the nations now on the earth. Few souls realize that one of the most important reasons for allowing the 'Time of the Nations,' as the recent phase of earth history is called, is to permit various states to pass through learning phases, and to set aside karma, in exactly the same way that human souls do. By observing the scenes taking place on the great stage of history, those who live on the earth can perceive on a grander scale the same process of learning and retribution which applies to human individuals.[3]

The pronouncements which Hilarion has given in relation to these 25 countries are quite telling. The opening statement for each country is the same. Such and such country has lost her _____. Each country has lost some quality or element of consciousness she once possessed. The only country which has not lost some positive quality of herself is Tibet. Tibet has lost her body, her physical body, whereas other nations have lost their compassion, their integrity, their perception, their honor, etc.

In relation to the destinies prophesied for those nations, Hilarion further explains the role and purpose of prophecy:

A final purpose for this booklet is to offer an exercise in prophecy to demonstrate that prophecy is a complex matter which can misfire, and that prophetic utterance should always be looked upon as if stating probabilities which may or may not come about, depending upon the reactions of those to whom the prophetic warning is delivered. True occultists have always understood that the best prophet is the false prophet, i.e. the one whose warnings of things to come have so impressed his listeners that they, by altering their hearts and minds, were able to avert the events which the prophet foresaw. Indeed, the only real justification for prophecy is the possibility that it will prompt those upon whose ears it falls to alter their lives for the better, and thus to improve their souls.[4]

America, too, has lost a quality she once had and also bears her own possible destiny. In the passage regarding America Hilarion has said: "This great country must have its rebirth along with all the rest. In many ways she is the greatest nation the earth has ever known. But she is flawed today by a blindness which has crept into her perception of the world..."[5]

The exact nature of that blindness and what it is within our character and personal make-up which would give rise to that flawed quality will be addressed in this Astrological analysis of the United States. My hope is that the message contained in these Astrological insights may go out to help clear away some of that blindness. My hope is that the future destiny towards which we are rapidly advancing may be lightened and attuned to a more positive role and mission, so that the more negative and painful possibilities before us may be dissolved in the light of a higher consciousness and perception.

1 Found in *Answer in the Sky,* by Sydney Omarr, p. 79.

2 The information which will be used extensively in this book was written and published by Maurice Cooke, in Ontario, Canada. The book containing this information is entitled: *Astrology Plus*. Mr. Cooke has published a series of books on a variety of subjects, known as the Hilarion Series. For those interested they may write the publisher directly. The address can be found in the appendix of this book.

3 *Nations,* Hilarion, P. 31.

4 Ibid, Pp. 31-32.

5 Ibid, P. 23.

UNDERSTANDING ASTROLOGY

As I mentioned in the Introduction I intend to present this discussion of the Astrological Birthchart of the U.S. in the same manner in which I would explain an Astrological chart to someone who has little or no prior knowledge of Astrology. To that end I will be presenting concepts which may be initially unfamiliar, but hopefully will afterwards be explained in more familiar terms. For those who wish to gain a more comprehensive understanding of the Astrological System I recommend the section in the Appendix which attempts to explain the basic functioning factors of Astrology. I would also recommend the many excellent Astrological texts now available to students of Astrology.

1

THE PLANET PLUTO AND THE SELF IMAGE
OF THE UNITED STATES

The paramount Astrological factor being affected during the events of September 11 was the 'Ascendant' of the U.S. birthchart. The Ascendant is the Astrological sign (of the twelve signs: Aries, Taurus, Gemini, etc.) situated on the eastern horizon at the time of birth. The sign which was 'rising' at the time of the birth of the United States of America was the sign Sagittarius. This Ascendant or 'Rising Sign' in a birthchart represents the self-image one has of oneself.

One significant impact of a Sagittarian Ascendant discerned by Hilarion is that:

> It will...give him a yearning to "see the world" through travel. There may even be in the self-picture some aspect of the "Wandering Jew" syndrome. In its effect upon the life, Sagittarius rising often delays marriage or causes there to be more than one marriage-like relationship, usually because of a tendency to cling to the youthfulness and adventurousness of the sign Sagittarius for many years after others have abandoned the excitement of their youthful dreams. This is not by any means to criticize the tendency of retaining a youthful outlook. Indeed, most people in the world now take up far too serious and heavy an attitude to life at an early age, turning their backs on the sense of fun and excitement which the Creator intended man to carry with him all his days.[1]

The U.S. is definitely a country with youthful dreams and enthusiasm. Author William Irwin Thompson, after moving from New York to Berne, Switzerland, remarked that the difference between New York and Berne is: "In New York, if you say you have an idea, everyone says 'Yeah, let's do it!' Whereas in Berne, if you say you have an idea, everyone says 'You can't do that!'

One could say that this youthful enthusiasm of the U.S. exists because we are so young compared to the European nations. However, all of the nations in North and South America are relatively young, and yet they do not display this same eager, at times even naive, enthusiasm of the U.S.

We are the nation which first developed the automobile, airplanes, and other vehicles of modern travel. Naturally, we would be the first to thrust men onto the Moon. People in other countries notice how much we travel or move from place to place. In 1959, when Hawaii was still only a territory of the U.S., and Hawaiians were voting for whether they wanted to become a state or not, the Hawaiians thought that becoming a state would increase tourism and thus their economy. However, they never imagined that continental, predominantly white Americans would actually want to *live* in Hawaii, so far from the roots of their family and communities. They did not grasp the deep rooted nature of American mobility, the willingness to seek new frontiers and boundaries. Of course this Sagittarian travel urge is a theme which has been present since our birth as seen in the sentiment of the commonly repeated phrase: 'Go West and seek your fortune young man.'

This Sagittarian travel and adventure idealism is one major element which would explain the national belief in our so-called 'Manifest Destiny'. This was, again, the belief in our Divinely Ordained destiny to expand our territorial boundaries to the Pacific shoreline. In this expansion there was a certain 'self-righteousness' in the faith that this was God's Will. A self-righteousness which made us capable of starting a war with Mexico, a war whose sole motive was territorial expansion. A self-righteousness which would decimate the destinies of the Native populations in our westward expansion, ignoring the promises we made in every treaty we ever made with those Native peoples. This self-righteousness, blind to the realities behind those actions we performed as we fulfilled our 'Divinely Ordained Manifest Destiny', is indicated by Hilarion's other commentary regarding Sagittarius on the Ascendant:

> This sign rising will tend to make the individual see himself as upright, honest and morally strong, *whether true or not*.[2] [Italics are mine]

Doesn't that sound like us? I'm sure it greatly confused and infuriated the Native Americans in their dealings with their 'Great White Father'.

In an essay *'The Manufacture of Consent,'* by Noam Chomsky he speaks of a gravestone he came across in a National Park with the following inscription: "Here lies an Indian woman, a Wampanoag, whose family and tribe gave of themselves and their land that this great nation might be born and grow."[3] Chomsky goes on to point out the obvious, that this tribe did not willingly self-sacrifice their existence for that noble purpose.

This Sagittarian self-image is what is particularly being confronted at this time. Although born and raised in the U.S., I have lived in most of the countries in Europe, and have traveled in the Middle East, South America and Asia. These periods abroad have provided me a deeper appreciation for life in the U.S., and a deeper awareness of how other nations perceive the U.S. I can honestly say that this arrogant, know-it-all, Sagittarian self-righteousness of the United State's character is the most universally despised aspect of ourselves. Resentment of this attitude has been expressed in every country I have ever been to.

A while after the events of September 11 I saw the following letter posted by a Canadian observer. I think it expresses a very prevalent sentiment outside of our borders:

> I have been struggling for the past few days with the need to say something here about how some of us in the rest of the world feel about what happened in New York. (That's pretty arrogant. How I and the people I talk to feel.) Or somehow put this into a perspective that isn't swept up in the growing American hysteria. I hesitated because it seemed like this was a mourning time, a time of waiting and watching and offering help and support. People here have felt an overwhelming need to do something—lines at blood banks in Vancouver are

around the block—people are leaving flowers at the US consulate, school children are sending teddy bears to children in NY schools—the malls are virtually deserted—our TV filled almost exclusively with coverage of the tragedy. We of course are mourning too. Many Canadians, Brits, Australians, Japanese are also missing and presumed dead. So please understand that what I have to say doesn't in any way negate the grief or the sympathy that we feel for those families who have suffered such terrible terrible losses.

But I notice that so much of what seems to be going on as people try to understand is a kind of "this isn't supposed to happen here" mentality. And I can't help asking, "Why not?" You are not unique. You may be the most powerful, indeed you are. You may have the most money. But that doesn't mean that you are somehow immune from the tragedies of the mess we have all made of this world. I find it mildly irritating every time I hear some commentator saying something about how Americans are pulling together and will survive because of their unique spirit. It's not the American spirit, it's the human spirit and it lives everywhere. Certainly if those planes had plowed into the CN tower in Toronto, or the Parliament buildings in Ottawa, Canadians would be responding exactly as Americans are. The difference would be that Americans wouldn't be watching 24 hour coverage of the incident on their television networks. When the Air India flight out of Toronto was blown out of the sky by terrorists ten years ago, and more than 500 people died, I wonder if there was more than a one minute news story on any American network.

Unfortunately the rest of the world understands America through the export of the worst part of its culture—movies, tv, fast food, guns and what we see is a nation utterly unable to comprehend itself as part of the world community. As a partner, an equal among equals. The rest of the world is pretty much invisible to you except as a backdrop against which to play out your interests. Canada, for example, is your biggest trading partner, shares with you the world's longest undefended border, but we are virtually unknown to you. I wonder how many Americans gave a shit about what's happening to the people of Afghanistan before all this happened. Or give a shit now—or recognize America's role in creating that horror.

Terrible tragedies happen all over the world all the time. This is not, as Bush said, the first war of the 21st century. There have already been several. They just didn't happen there so for him, they don't count.

Are there people in the US who do care about the rest of the world? Of course—thoughtful, informed, caring people— many of them here in this forum. But that's not the image we have. That's not what we see in the cultural barrage flowing out from your borders every day. Our images are of violence— school shootings, executions, invasions—and of mindless consumption—bigger cars, bigger malls, bigger dumps.

America wants to be the biggest, the toughest—and it is. That's its strength, but it's also its weakness. The guy who swaggers around the school yard, occasionally giving some poor squirt who annoyed him a bloody nose is inevitably going to be challenged. And somebody will, sooner or later, give him a bloody nose back. And the poor squirt who got beat up last week, will probably be glad it happened.

You can blow Afghanistan up, probably will—you can put armed guards on airplanes, and seal the borders and impose economic sanctions. But it won't solve the problem. We are all vulnerable because, like it or not, we all live in the same world.[4]

As I said, this is a common sentiment among the many nations I have visited. The part of the Sagittarian self-image which we most strongly have to confront is that we do continually see ourselves as honest, upright, and morally strong, *whether true or not*. The fact is there are times when we truly are honest, upright, and morally strong. If we look back to that day of July 4, 1776, the day of the signing of the Declaration of Independence, we would witness the establishment of one of the strongest moral documents in history. In the Astrological system, the sign of the Ascendant changes approximately every two hours. The local time used for the moment of the signing of the

Declaration in the Sibley chart is 5:10 PM. One could say that before 4:00 PM, or after 6:00 PM, there would have been a different sign, a different self-image operative at that time. The tale is told that the Declaration had been written, but it took until late in the afternoon for those present to sign it, for to do so was to place their lives in jeopardy of death. A death which would come as a result of a pronouncement of a British court for the crime of high treason. My sense is the men in that room had to wait until the optimism, enthusiasm, honesty and true moral righteousness of the sign Sagittarius was rising on the eastern horizon before they could commit themselves, as it says in the last sentence of the Declaration: 'And for the support of this declaration, with a firm reliance on the protection of Divine Providence, we mutually pledge to each other our lives, our fortunes, and our sacred honor.'

The positive force and spirit embodied in the birth of this country is readily apparent in the Astrological chart of this country. These positive qualities, operative in the birth of this nation, will be examined in the next chapter. However, in relation to this Sagittarian self-image, there is a very forceful Astrological 'challenge' bearing down upon it at this time. It is this challenge which has set events in motion to change our view of our nation. These events will induce us to bridge the gap between what we see as morally strong behavior and what other nations see as otherwise. Before we look at the details of that Astrological challenge I would like to share what Hilarion has said about America in his book *Nations:*

America has lost her generosity.

Once, when the world was groaning in the aftermath of a great and terrible war, she stood forth with her riches in her hand, offering them freely to those who had been broken by the strife. She did not refuse to give of herself, of her wealth, of her energy and of her love. What Europe has become today is largely a result of the generosity of the American spirit and the ideals of brotherhood which this country has held so high.

But today America has drawn back and has closed the door to

other nations. She has sealed herself behind a wall and refuses to offer help to those less fortunate than herself.

This great country must have its rebirth along with all the rest. In many ways she is the greatest nation the earth has ever known. But she is flawed today by a blindness which has crept into her perception of the world.[5]

An interesting example of the effects of our short-sighted, self-enclosed blindness involves one of the terrorists connected to the U.S. Embassy bombing in Kenya in 1998. He had grown up on one of the small undeveloped Muslim islands in the Persian Gulf. When he graduated from secondary school there were no opportunities for further study where he was living. There had been a U.S. foreign aid program which helped students like him pursue further studies, even enabling some to come and study in the U.S. When most of the U.S. foreign aid programs were cut, his academic choices were reduced to attending an Islamic fundamentalist university in Saudi Arabia. There he unfortunately became an Islamic extremist, went to Afghanistan, and became a terrorist. If, at that earlier juncture, he had been able to attend school in the U.S., or anywhere besides a fundamentalist Islamic University, his likely choices in life would have been different.

Plutonian Confrontation

The Astrological force now bearing upon the self-image of the U.S., which has the capability of removing that 'blindness' in our 'perception of the world,' involves the planet Pluto. It takes Pluto 247 years to go around the Zodiacal circle of twelve Astrological signs. In the year 2023 it will return to the position which it occupied at the time of the birth of our nation. Here are some of Hilarion's comments regarding Pluto:

> The Planet Pluto is the great bringer of change. Where this planet is located in the birth chart always designates an area or department of life in which the soul has agreed to undergo pressures promoting a deep-seated alteration in its attitudes, habits or understanding. If the personality resists these pres-

sures, then much stress and difficulty will be felt. Pluto is like the irresistible force, sweeping all before it. The only beneficial approach to this planet's energies is to move in the direction it indicates. To do otherwise is to invite disaster.[6]

The influence of 'transiting' Pluto on our Sagittarian self-image was in effect on September 11, 2001. Transits are the effects upon a birthchart from the various planets as they move in the sky. As the planets move in their orbits they form different kinds of 'aspects' which include conjunctions (where the planet in the sky is in the same position as the placement in the chart), squares and oppositions (essentially tense aspects, forming angles of 90 and 180 degrees respectively) and trines and sextiles (harmonious, mutually supportive aspects of 120 and 60 degrees).

In the year 2000 the planet Pluto, this great bringer of change, transited to the exact degree and minute of our Sagittarian Ascendant for the first time since our nation's birth. In that year Pluto made three exact conjunctions on January 31, April 30, and November 25. The third of those conjunctions, in November of 2000, was when the political fate of our country of 281 million people hinged upon the disputed resolution of 537 votes. Our whole nation was in 'limbo' at that time. It seemed to me that this could not be a mere accident, that there was a message in our being stopped in our political 'tracks'. The question is what was the message? Both political parties, seeing themselves as honest, upright and morally strong, *whether true or not*, were left hanging over a yawning Plutonian chasm of fated uncertainty. On September 11, 2001, Pluto was within 17 minutes of arc away from the exact degree and minute of the Sagittarian Ascendant of the U.S. The ramifications of Pluto, bringing massive changes to our Sagittarian self-image and perspective are profound and extensive.

After conjuncting the Ascendant of our birthchart in November, Pluto has moved for some time into our first 'house'. Houses represent arenas of activity for the functioning of the various planets. The first house is the house of self-image or personality. Pluto will be in that house until approximately 2018. For this next period of years our self-image of ourselves is going to go through complete death/rebirth.

Personally, I think 9/11 was a Plutonian 'wake-up call' for this country. Pluto is the planet which makes you look at what are your true motivations. Is it love and faith in yourself and life and the Higher Power behind life? Or is it fear and lack of faith in yourself and life and the Higher Power behind life? Our youthful, naive innocence, our immaturity, and our impudent self-righteousness are being asked to grow up fast. Another commentary regarding Pluto by Hilarion states:

> The changes indicated by Pluto...are unavoidable and can be absolutely counted on to take place. In the case of most individuals, the changes come about "by force", i.e. they are resisted by the individual and must be rammed home by the implacable and irresistible force of events. When resistance is shown to such changes, the experiences are inevitably harder and more painful than they would have been if the individual had "seen the writing on the wall" as it were, and had voluntarily stepped in the direction in which the events were trying to move him.[7]

Here are some additional comments from Hilarion relative to both Canada and America. This commentary acknowledges the positive foundations of both of these nations and yet proclaims the need for a 'reawakening':

North America has lost its roots.

> This paradise was deliberately created on the earth to be the new Atlantis, a rich garden into which humanity's most evolved fraction would be allowed to incarnate. The twin nations of Canada and the United States have been carefully guided from higher planes through all of their initial phases, to ensure that godliness, honour and moral rectitude would lie at the very foundation of their national structures. The laws which protect the individual from coercion by others and the constitutions which shield him from the oppression of government, are bulwarks against the erosion of liberty that has stained so many other countries. The traditions of freedom in this oasis shine out like a great flame for the rest of the darkened planet, showing all who can still see truth that slavery need not be the lot of humanity...

Yet that flame shines not as it once did. In times past, the consciousness of the North American people clung to these traditions of liberty and equality with great tenacity, and through their steadfastness a wondrous ray of light from the Eternal was anchored into the land where these nations stand. But now that consciousness has dimmed, as the evil root of greed and self-seeking has pushed all nobler concerns into the background.

Soon there will be a reawakening. The traditions of fairness and freedom will come alive again, but this time with an added awareness: that the human family is destined to reunite itself in brotherhood and caring, and that *love* must now lie at the basis of all that mankind undertakes.

The time is not far off. Though the path must first wind through a season of sorrow and shock for the race, yet all who steadfastly cling to the light of God's countenance will find their feet at last stepping forth into His eternal gardens of praise, where tears are shed only for happiness, and the laughter of His children fills every dancing day with joy[8]

That 'season of sorrow and shock for the race' is something Hilarion refers to as the 'Tribulation', a period of testing and trial for the whole planet. This is something which has been prophesied in many different spiritual prophecies. I will share my perspective of what Hilarion has said in regard to the Tribulation at the end of this book. Suffice it to say here that we will all, individually and collectively, be going through this period of testing and trial of human life on this planet.

The element of material greed pointed out by Hilarion is, to me, so obvious and yet so seemingly far off of our national radar screen. As I write this, the Enron Corporation scandal is being investigated by Congress, the courts and the media. The Enron Corporation made political campaign contributions to 71 of 100 senators, and yet paid no taxes in 4 of the last 5 years.

It may be apparent that my personal political sentiments lie somewhere left of center, and yet there is much of the left wing of American politics which also bears the negative image of this Sagittarian Ascendant. Seeing this factor in the U.S. birthchart has given me new vocabulary for what I have long observed. This tendency towards self-righteousness is something which permeates virtually all of American society, left and right. It is rather easy to point it out when it is as blatant as some of the statements coming out of the mouths of people like Jerry Falwell and Pat Robertson. However, I, personally, also have a hard time with people who are so invested into their resentment of the negative aspects of this country that they have more compassion for Osama Bin Laden than they do for George Bush. To me fanaticism is fanaticism.

After my lecture in Eugene, Oregon, a woman said to me that she wouldn't go to a vigil for the victims at the World Trade Center because she never went to a vigil for the victims in Afghanistan or Malaysia. Why should she go to a vigil for the victims at the World Trade Center just because it was in her own country? I can understand the sentiment. I think that we should have more sensitivity to what happens outside of our own borders. I am also aware of the high degree of hypocrisy in this country. A country which decries the heinous terrorism on its own shores, while having used the CIA to help undermine a legitimately elected, but socialist leaning democratic government in Chile, to put in place the 'friendly' government of the military dictator Pinochet, a man who murdered 5-10,000 individuals. (Curiously, the coup took place on September 11, 1973.) Nonetheless, when that woman in Eugene expressed her disregard for the World Trade Center victims, all I could feel afterwards was 'Where is your heart and human compassion?' We Americans get so attached to our 'party-line,' whether left or right, that we tend to lose our human heart and compassion.

In the opening to an article entitled "An End to Sweet Illusions" by Bill McKibben, relating to post 9/11 America, he states:

"War is hell to figure out, and so its usual effect is to simplify our thinking. It's either hit 'em harder, they deserve it (mainstream thought), or this is wrong and stupid (left variant). But these last few months have felt different—people aren't reacting quite as reflexively as usual. We seem to be struggling toward reality".[9]

In relation to the more mainstream left, I think the most coherent comments were expressed by Marianne Williamson in her excellent book: *The Healing of America*:

Those who actually attack the cause of social justice have a way of stirring us to action. Those who give it mere lip service have a way of lulling us to sleep.[10]

The question following 9/11 is whether this event will stir us to action, of the right kind, or whether we will allow ourselves to be lulled back to sleep. Pluto, now bearing upon that self-image of possible self-righteous self-deception, will force us, sooner or later, to see in what ways we are truly motivated by love and by our higher, more evolved selves, and where we are motivated by fear and self-interest and by our lower, less-evolved selves.

Again quoting from '*An End to Sweet Illusions*':

Look—Osama bin Laden's actions have clearly been those of a maniac, and it has clearly been necessary to get rid of him. That is realistic, and that's why there haven't been crowds in the street opposing the war in Afghanistan. But getting rid of him won't end our insecurity, and the ways in which we take him on could make us more vulnerable, not less. That is realistic, and that's why Americans aren't cheering on this war with our usual fervor.

Realism is a bore and a bother. It's infinitely nicer to live in a world of illusion—that we were different from other nations, that we could ignore international agreements that didn't suit us, that we could go on using cheap energy without ever paying a price. Our success and our geographic isolation have let us get away with those delusions, but September 11 has shown them for what they were. Hence the need for real realism, for a view more clear-eyed and hard-nosed than we've had before.[11]

Sagittarian Enthusiasm Or Fanaticism

Sagittarius is the sign related to philosophy, religion, and higher mental pursuits. Pluto moving through Sagittarius is going to transform religions and people's belief systems throughout the world. It will bring dark elements up from the underworld to be consciously recognized and healed. This can be seen in Pope John Paul's efforts to review the dark epochs of the Catholic Church, such as the Inquisition as well as its shameful treatment of Orthodox Christians and Jews.

However, the shadow side of the sign Sagittarius is fanaticism. Pluto is going to bring this out of the underworld for us to review as well. Our Sagittarian self-image has made us particularly susceptible to being involved in the abuse of fanatical belief systems. The time period when Pluto first dipped into the sign Sagittarius, for a span of 94 days, before going back into Scorpio for several more months, was the same period of time during which Timothy McVeigh blew up the Federal building in Oklahoma City in 1995.

The rise of fanatical anti-government groups in the U.S. accelerated after the end of the Cold War in 1989. This may be explained by the fact that Sagittarius needs to feel enthusiastic and impassioned about something. The two greatest motives for excitement and passion are love and hate. My sense of many of those drawn to the militia groups is that these are people who thrive on having an enemy. During the Cold War these people focused their hate on the Communists. Now that we no longer have the Communists as clear cut enemies, our own government becomes the enemy. Unfortunately our government acted out its own Sagittarian self-righteous fanaticism in its 'Rambo' style actions in the assault on religious cult leader David Koresh's compound in Waco, Texas. Fanaticism is fanaticism. As Mahatma Gandhi said: 'An eye for an eye makes the whole world blind'.

America's need for an enemy to focus its energies upon is also related to the influence of having the planet Mars in the Seventh house. The Seventh House is the house related to the experience of partnerships and relationships and we will examine this influence in a later chapter.

In the meantime it is apparent that Pluto has put our Sagittarian traits on the world stage.

The possibility that our Sagittarian enthusiasm could, once again, serve the cause of love, compassion and sincere care for others is there in our birthchart. I am happy to see it there. It helps me keep faith in the future of this country. Faith that the blindness upon us will come away and we will be able to see that, as Hilarion said: "*love* must now lie at the basis of all that mankind undertakes".

1   *Astrology Plus*, pp. 27-28.
2   Ibid, p. 27.
3   Found in *War Talk*, by Arundhati Roy, p. 86.
4   Written by Bonnie Evans, published on the forum: *The Well*, at www.salon.com
5   *Nations*, p. 23.
6   *Astrology Plus*., p. 155.
7   Ibid. p. 77.
8   *Nations*., p.24.
9   *An End to Sweet Illusions*, Mother Jones Magazine, January, 2002, p. 38.
10   *The Healing of America*, Marianne Williamson, p. 125.
11   *An End to Sweet Illusions*, Bill McKibben, Mother Jones Magazine, January 2002, p. 39.

2

The Birth of the United States of America

The placement of the Moon in an Astrological birthchart indicates the relative influence of that individual's childhood in their prospective life. The Moon in the birthchart for the United States is in the sign of Aquarius. The energies of this sign of Aquarius were the main influence during the birth and early life of this country.

Since the 1960's, virtually everyone has heard of the coming of the 'Age of Aquarius'. This sense of an entire age or period of history being assigned to the influence of a particular sign has to do with what is referred to as the 'Precession of the Equinoxes'. This 'precession' describes the Astrological constellation of stars directly behind the Sun on the first day of Spring, the Spring Equinox, and their projected movement through the signs of the 'Zodiac'. It takes approximately 2,160 years for this 'precession' to move through one complete sign. It takes 25,820 years to complete one full cycle of the Zodiac. The gradual cosmic pace of this 'precession' inevitably impacts the course of civilizations far more than the meteoric rise and fall of individuals.

The period of the past 2,000 years or so has been designated the Piscean Age. The symbol for Pisces is two fishes swimming in opposite directions. Pisces is ruled by the planet Neptune, god or goddess of the sea. Piscean symbolism has been related to the experience of Christianity of the past 2,000 years. Early Christians used the symbol of the fish as an emblem of their secret faith. Jesus walked on the sea and was referred to as a 'fisher of men'. In the Piscean era, the Christian religion involved a Neptunian quality of mystical faith and surrender. This is best symbolized by Jesus' test of faith and subsequent surrender in the Garden of Gethsemene, leading to his Crucifixion and the Neptunian transcendence of physical law with his resurrection.

The fact that our modern secular society, in this last portion of the Piscean Age, bears little evidence of this kind of Piscean/Neptunian mystical faith and surrender is due to the fact that everything at this level of manifestation appears as a duality. Opposite to the sign Pisces is the sign Virgo, representing the analytical mind and practical, technical capabilities. A duality between the influence of these two signs has been the theme of the past two millennia.

A good example of this duality is illustrated in the opposing views of how life originated on earth. The evolutionists champion Darwin's 'survival of the fittest' and a material, rational explanation for evolution, whereas the 'creationists' ardently believe in the literal 'word of God' such that God created everything in seven days. The hallmark of the Pisces/Virgo age has been that people tended to occupy one camp or the other. Either they were faith dependent and refuting concrete practical law, or they were strictly rational, materially identified, and negating the possibility of any reality beyond what can be objectively known and verified. The shift from an earlier era of faith and surrender to the present technocratic secularism reveals the enduring division between Pisces and Virgo.

One could say that the experience of the conflict of duality seems to be an inevitable part of life at this plane of existence. An obvious resolution to this particular Pisces/Virgo duality is for one to be able to embrace and integrate both realities. It would comprise of accepting that there is a concrete, logical basis to life, as well as a clear requirement for some kind of mystical intervention.

The ability to embrace both views will characterize the qualities of the coming Aquarian Age. Hilarion suggests it will usher in a new universal religion based on experience rather than solely on faith. There is a current teaching that the coming New Age will be the marriage of Science and Religion. This would represent the integration of the energies released in the past Piscean/Virgoan epoch. There are presently individuals using scientific inquiry to examine age-old mystical practices. Science itself has crossed the threshold into mysticism with its investigation of quantum physics.

Aquarius is the sign related to the experience of group consciousness and the Universal Brotherhood of Mankind, or the Universal Brother/Sisterhood of Humankind. Aquarius is 'ruled' by the planet Uranus, the planet of freedom, of sudden change out of the blue which you didn't expect. The concrete existence of Uranus was discovered in the year 1781, a few months before the end of the conflict of the American Revolution, and eight years before the French Revolution.

Nearly all of the early founders of the United States, as well as significant individuals who would later exert profound influence upon this country, were marked, in some way, by the sign Aquarius. This is what Hilarion says regarding an individual born under the sign Aquarius:

> The Aquarian is one who, in a prior life, dedicated his energies to bringing others together into a united group and encouraging love and brotherhood between them. Because the peacemaker is to be honored above all others in spiritual terms, the Aquarian is allowed a special tap into a source of the highest idealism regarding the brotherhood of man, both at the soul level and at the personality level, filters permitting. But this source of ideal brotherhood represents a level of advancement far beyond the achievements of the race to the present day. Love is not universally felt for all; indeed, the only circumstance in which most individuals get even a glimpse of love in its true majesty is that first overwhelming excitement of the love affair, before the cold realities show themselves. But the Aquarian knows instinctively that the universal non-exclusive love is possible, and this often introduces a problem in relating to others at the level which mankind has reached.[1]

The Moon in Aquarius of the United States is positively aspected, for which Hilarion says:

The more positively aspected the Moon in this sign, the more the positive aspects of encouragement of individuality and independent thinking will be found.[2]

The declarations and energies instrumental in the founding of the United States involved an encouragement of individuality and independent thinking. The Aquarian energy was embodied in many of our founding fathers. George Washington was a Pisces, yet born only two days after the month of Aquarius. Aquarius was also the sign in which was placed his Mercury, representing the mental, thinking, and communicating aspect of his personality. Washington also had an Aquarian 'Mid-Heaven,' the sign which was directly overhead when he was born, which represents how he would have presented himself to, and interacted with, the world.

Thomas Jefferson was an Aries, but his Ascendant, or self-image, was Aquarius. Benjamin Franklin was a Capricorn, but in the sign Aquarius he had Mercury, representing his mental, thinking qualities. The Polish revolutionary Thaddeus Kosciuszko, who fought in the American and Polish revolutionary efforts, was an Aquarian. He also had in the sign Aquarius both Venus and also Uranus, the planet ruling Aquarius. Kosciuszko's desire for universal brotherhood was expressed again in his will, where he left instructions to sell his property and use the proceeds to purchase the freedom of slaves.

Perhaps the most significant and yet underrated Aquarian individual in the founding of our country was the inspired revolutionary writer Thomas Paine. He was born with his Sun in Aquarius. He also had Mercury and Jupiter 'conjunct' in Aquarius. For Jupiter in Aquarius Hilarion says:

> Jupiter in this sign of brotherhood points to the ability to bring together conflicting groups, to forge closer ties between people and to promote universal good-will and love. The expression of this ability is the highest calling of the person with Jupiter in Aquarius. [3]

One could say that Thomas Paine was the most Aquarian of all the founding fathers. Having his Jupiter conjunct his Mercury would lead him to express those Aquarian ideals through writing, speaking and communicating. His Jupiter is 'trine,' or positively aspecting, Neptune, attuning this Aquarian energy with spiritual faith and surrender. Paine's Jupiter is also trine to Pluto, providing the ability to use this Aquarian idealism and communication as a means of profound transformation.

A brief synopsis of the involvement of Thomas Paine in the revolutionary birth of our country sheds light upon the strong Aquarian influence he brought to bear in the founding of our country. The essentials of this synopsis come from the book *'America's Invisible Guidance,'* by Corinne Heline. In the early 1770's Paine was arrested in London for stating that monarchies should be ended and all people made free and equal. Benjamin Franklin was in London at the time and helped Paine move to Britain's North American colonies. Once relocated, Paine began writing articles 'urging abolition of war and peace settlements by international arbitration; advocating international copyright laws and declaring that women should not be bound by "indissoluble ties"; denouncing cruelty to animals and asserting that monarchies and hereditary titles were anachronisms.'[3]

Following the Boston Tea Party in 1773, Paine started writing his famous essay 'Common Sense'. It was published on January 17, 1776, three days before the Sun went into Aquarius. One hundred thousand copies were sold in three months, an unheard of amount in Colonial America or anywhere at that time. George Washington noted its powerful effect on the 'minds and hearts of men'. Writer Joel Barlow declared that "America owes as much to the pen of Paine as to the sword of Washington".

Looking now at some of Paine's Aquarian Age statements which were numerous and prophetic:

The birthday of the new world is at hand. There has not been a like condition since the days of Noah. It is in our power to begin the world over again.

To see it in our power to make a world happy, to teach mankind the art of being so, to exhibit, on the theatre of the universe, a character hitherto unknown, and to have, as it were, a new creation entrusted to our hands, are honors that demand reflection, and can neither be too highly estimated, nor too gratefully received.

Begin by giving to all the true hand of friendship. Draw a line of oblivion to bury every former dissension. Let no party name of Whig or Tory be heard among us, only that of good citizen, resolute friend and vigorous supporter of the rights of mankind and of the free and independent states of America.

It has been surmised that Thomas Paine and Thomas Jefferson, working together, wrote the Declaration of Independence. Author Manly P. Hall, contends that it was probably Paine who wrote the entire document, later submitting it to Jefferson for editing and revision. Hall points out that concepts in the Declaration, such as "the Laws of Nature" and "Nature's God", represented Paine's theological beliefs.

In the winter of 1776 Washington's army was in dire straights due to lack of food and clothing. Many of the Continental Army's volunteer soldiers died from the cold and illness. The well equipped and outfitted British mercenaries inflicted defeat after defeat. The patriots' morale plummeted and desertions rose alarmingly high. General Washington was forced to retreat, making his famous crossing of the Delaware on December 7, 1776 . British General Howe was able to easily capture the prized city of Philadelphia. On December 19, 1776 Paine wrote *The Crisis* and it was immediately published in *The Pennsylvania Journal*. Corinne Heline says: "Its opening words soon became the battle cry of the new republic:

These are times which try men's souls…Tyranny, like hell, is not easily conquered. The harder the conflict the more glorious the victory. That which is won too cheaply is esteemed too lightly. Heaven knows how to put the proper price upon its goods and it would be strange indeed if so celestial an article as Freedom be not highly rated.

Paine's inspirational words restored hope and aspiration to the beleaguered patriots. Members of the Continental army who had deserted came back. General Washington ordered that *The Crisis* be read each morning to his troops. Shortly afterwards the rejuvenated Americans rallied with the convincing victories at Princeton and Trenton.

In the following month Paine published the second issue of *The Crisis* which the public eagerly devoured. Paine boldly proclaimed the name of the new country then being born: The United States of America. Paine's Aquarian regard for universal brotherhood was further expressed in an article, *'The Proclamation of the Abolition of Slavery,'* published in 1779. This was the first article to argue for the ending of slavery ever published in this country.

After the American Revolution, Paine went to France to encourage the establishment of democracy in that nation. While there he wrote volumes One and Two of *The Rights of Man*. In 1792, among other visionary pronouncements, Paine put forth arguments for the establishment of what we now know as Social Security: "Use the money now spent on war in this way. It is painful in so-called civilized countries to see old age working itself to death. Pensions are not to be given as matters of grace and favor, but as rights."

In the preface to the second volume of *The Rights of Man*, Paine declared:

> The revolution of America presented in politics what was only theory in mechanics. So deeply rooted were all the governments of the old world, and so effectually had the tyranny and the antiquity of habit established itself over the mind, that no beginning could be made in Asia, Africa, or Europe, to reform the political condition of man. Freedom had been hunted round the globe; reason was considered as rebellion; and the slavery of fear had made men afraid to think.

> But such is the irresistible nature of truth, that all it asks, and all it wants, is the liberty of appearing. The sun needs no inscription to distinguish him from darkness; and no sooner did the

American governments display themselves to the world, than despotism felt a shock, and man began to contemplate redress.

The independence of America, considered merely as a separation from England, would have been a matter but of little importance, had it not been accompanied by a revolution in the principles and practice of governments. She made a stand, not for herself only, but for the world, and looked beyond the advantages herself could receive.

Paine's radical ideas later led to his vilification by the very masses for whom he struggled. In the words of Corinne Heline: "Hated by the Royalists and too advanced to be appreciated even by the democracies whom he was dedicated to serve, he stood a target for persecution on both sides of the Atlantic." This is in resonance with what Hilarion said regarding those born with the Sun in Aquarius: "... the Aquarian knows instinctively that the universal non-exclusive love is possible, and this often introduces a problem in relating to others at the level which mankind has reached. "

Ms. Heline said that Thomas Paine's own words would best serve as his epitaph: "The world is my country and to do good is my religion."

This Aquarian energy, embodied in Thomas Paine and other founding fathers of this nation, seems to reappear when crisis requires the U.S. to realign itself with its original visions. For example, the 'captains of the ship' of America during the Civil War and the Great Depression, Abraham Lincoln and Franklin D. Roosevelt, were both born with their Sun in Aquarius.

The fact that a strong, cutting, intellectual force, as well as a strong militaristic force, would play a part in the birth of our country, is indicated by the fact that the Moon in our birthchart is 'trine,' in positive aspect to the planet Mars. The Moon trine to Mars, in itself, would represent a positive, effective experience of dynamic, courageous, and willful energy, with successful results. This is apparent in the military victory of the colonials against the greatest military power in the world at that time. The intellectual effort accommodating that victory would be due to the fact that our Mars is in Gemini, for which Hilarion says:

> This sign [Gemini] is a mental one, ruled by Mercury, and Mars here will tend to express its energies through the mental gifts. There will be considerable mental energy present, if the positive aspects to Mars can be found.

This positive mental effort in alignment with Aquarian ideals is evident in the various documents at the heart of the creation of this nation. The Declaration of Independence, the Constitution, and the Bill of Rights are all powerful intellectual expressions of Aquarian ideals.

The Masons

In addition to the Aquarian inspiration of Thomas Paine and other founders of our nation, there are two very important, yet rarely mentioned sources of the new visionary ideals that inspired the birth of this country.

The existence of the first of these sources emerged into the public consciousness in 1935, at a time when democracy was under siege from dictatorships around the world. For the first time the image of the reverse side of the Great Seal of the United States, originally created in 1782, was revealed to the American public. This image consists of an eye in a triangle, suspended above a pyramid which is missing its capstone. Above are the words: Annuit Coeptis (God favors this undertaking). Below are the words: Novo Ordo Seclorum (New Order of the Ages). Since 1935 this side of our Great Seal has been printed on our $1 bills.

The obverse side of the Seal features the well known Eagle, grasping the olive branch of peace in one clawed foot, and the arrows of war in the other. This side of the Seal was familiar to Americans since it had been cast into metal prior to 1935. The symbolism of this side of the Seal follows traditional elements of heraldic tradition. However, the reverse side of the seal, with its single eye in a triangle and pyramid, depicts symbolism usually understood only by members of so-called secret societies, such as the Freemasons, Rosicrucians, etc. These symbolic images, designed in 1792, were elevated into national consciousness in 1935 largely through the efforts of Henry Wallace and FDR, both members of Masonic orders. It is well documented that many, if not most, of the signers of the Declaration of Independence, the generals and officers in Washington's Army, and also the members of the First Continental Congress were Freemasons.

There are obvious reasons as to why the Masonic brotherhoods would ably serve the cause of the American Revolution. First, the levels of secrecy and trust required for the successful planning of an insurrection, while risking death for high treason, already existed within these brotherhoods. Second, the Masonic Lodges historically espoused freedom of religious worship for all forms of religion. They practiced tolerance of religious diversity even though their particular guiding light, placed upon the Masonic altar, was the Bible. The Masonic Lodges served as a protective umbrella for the diverse religious faiths flourishing within the American colonies. The Mason's defense of religious freedom in America is consistent with their traditional opposition to the authoritative tyrannies of the European monarchies and the established Protestant and Catholic Churches.

The third, and unacknowledged reason, why the Masonic Societies would support our Revolution is revealed in their underlying purpose. The spiritual evolution and advancement of mankind is what these societies have long labored in secret to accomplish. In the extensively documented books *The Secret Destiny of America* and *America's Assignment with Destiny* by Manly P. Hall, and *America's Invisible Guidance* by Corinne Heline, the authors demonstrate that members of these brotherhoods skillfully cultivated the vision of a new society and a novel form of government, a truly 'New Order of the Ages,' on our continent since the 1600's. This effort has been made in league with the segment of humanity which operates from higher planes of being, the so-called Ascended Masters of the Spiritual Hierarchy.

Whether these societies presently maintain the same vision and 'inner plane contacts' with the Spiritual Hierarchy they once did is hard to gauge. What remains of Masonic practice appears to employ the same symbols used in ritual during previous centuries. However, one may surmise that the membership, over the past two hundred years, has suffered, as has society in general, from the same enemies of spiritual belief and advancement: scientific materialism and skepticism. As a result it seems that the Masonic orders function today more as humanistic, fraternal societies, and less in the mystical, spiritually attuned capacities they once did. As Manly P. Hall states:

> The old adversaries were gone. The power of the Church and State to plague the destiny of the average man was broken. It was no longer needful to struggle against the despotism of feudalism or the perversities of princes. The Inquisition had lost its terror, and theology was unable to impose its traditional formulas upon a down-trodden laity. But the ills that men must bear changed their appearances, not their substance. The authority of science took the place left vacant by the departing authorities of aristocracy and theology. It was still necessary for the human spirit to struggle against the intolerances of the human mind.[4]

With a greater understanding of the involvement of these secret societies let us now revisit the Masonic influence upon the design of the reverse side of the Great Seal. Freemasonry traces the origin of their brotherhoods back to ancient Egypt. The Pyramid on the reverse side of our Great Seal is claimed by some to represent the tomb of Hermes, the god of Wisdom. Others contend the Pyramid depicts a Chamber of Initiation, symbolizing the death of identification with the four-sided square of material reality, and the rebirth within the point of oneness with divine consciousness, thereby awakening the all-seeing eye of Horus.

The symbolism of the reverse side of the Seal was explained by Charles Thomson and William Barton, officials of the third and final committee assigned to the design of the seal:

> The pyramid signifies Strength and Duration: The Eye over it & the Motto allude to the many signal interpositions of providence in favor of the American cause. The date underneath is

that of the Declaration of Independence and the words under it signify the beginning of the new American Era, which commences from that date.[5]

Others interpret the imagery to illustrate that providence and divine inspiration must guide the structure of our society. Otherwise *Annuit Coeptis*, the prospering of our efforts by the Divine will fail to occur. Likewise, our mission to establish a 'Novo Ordo Seclorum,' a New Order of the Ages, for ourselves and for our planet, would also fail.

The Eagle-imprinted side has been used to stamp national documents, thus manifesting, symbolically and concretely, the signature of our country. The fact that the reverse side has never been used as an actual stamp may indicate that the true fulfillment of our destiny is only half completed. As a nation we have manifested the lofty and powerful Eagle, struggling between the embrace of peace and the acceptance of war. However, as a nation, we have not yet fully developed a consciousness that reflects a oneness with Divine Guidance. If the structure of our society were in harmony with the Divine we could manifest the biblical injunction in the bible in Matthew 6:22 : 'If therefore, thine eyes be single thy whole body shall be full of light'. [6]

Native Americans

The other generally unrecognized source influencing the quality and structure of the United States came from the interaction between certain members of the colonists and branches of Native American society. In the publications, *Indian Givers: How the Indians of America Transformed the World*, by Jack Weatherford, and *America's Secret Destiny*, by Robert Hieronimus, Ph.D., this interaction has been well presented. Of particular significance is the interaction of the colonists and the League of the Iroquois, a federation of six tribes in what is now the Northeastern U.S. This federation was created somewhere between 1000 and 1450 AD. A contemporary of Benjamin Franklin described the Iroquois Federation:

[The Indians} have "outdone the Romans"...[They have} a social and political system so old that the immigrant Europeans knew nothing of its origins — a federal union of five (and later six) Indian nations that had put into practice concepts of popular participation and natural rights that the European savants had thus far only theorized. The Iroquoian system, expressed through its constitution "The Great Law of Peace," rested on assumptions foreign to monarchies of Europe: it regarded leaders as servants of the people, rather than their masters, and made provision for their leaders' impeachment for errant behavior. The Iroquois' law and custom upheld freedom of expression in political and religious matters and it forbade the unauthorized entry of homes. It provided for political participation by women and relatively equitable distribution of wealth...[7]

In 1744 the Iroquois chief Canassatego was the first to suggest that the individual colonies unify themselves into a federated union. Canassatego put forth this suggestion because he and other Indians were finding it difficult to deal with all of the different, individual governing bodies of the separate colonies. Benjamin Franklin served as the Indian commissioner for the colony of Pennsylvania. In 1751 he wrote:

The colonists should accept the Iroquois advice to form a union in common defense under a common, federal government...It would be a very strange thing if six nations of ignorant savages should be capable of forming a scheme for such an Union and be able to execute it in such a manner as that it has subsisted ages, and appears indissoluble, and yet a like union should be impracticable for ten or a dozen English colonies. [8]

According to Jack Weatherford the colonists' initial descriptions of the Native Americans routinely expressed: "amazement at the Indians' personal liberty, in particular their freedom from rulers and from social classes based on ownership of property. For the first time the French and the British became aware of the possibility of living in social harmony and prosperity without the rule of a king."[9] Thomas Paine served as secretary to the Colonial commissioners who negotiated with the Iroquois. He decried the abusive treatment of the Indians by the British. In his book *Agrarian Justice*, which addressed the poverty produced by the 'civilized society' of Europe, Paine wrote: "The fact is, that the condition of millions, in every country in Europe, is far worse than if they had been born before civilization began, or had been born among the Indians of North-America at the present day."[10]

The Iroquois constitution was called the *Kaianerekowa*, or Great Law of Peace. Many key elements of the *Kaianerekowa* were incorporated into the structure of our own Constitution. Our federal government is based on the Iroquois model of several sovereign governing bodies unified into an over-all governing body. This overall governing body dealt with issues of common interest to all of the individual tribal nations. The leaders of this governing body were elected, instead of being selected by hereditary lineage. The Iroquois also practiced the separation of power between governing officials and military officials, by prohibiting persons from serving in both capacities simultaneously. The Iroquois model of government also provided for the option of impeachment if any 'sachem,' or leader, failed to properly perform their duty. Our founding fathers adopted each of these Iroquois innovations in constructing our Constitution. Unfortunately, these men lacked the vision to also adopt the Iroquois practice of allowing women to vote.

This positive influence of Native American society upon our nation has traditionally gone unnoticed by most U.S. historians. The shameful record of White European interaction with Native Americans since the birth of our nation is a subject which must be confronted in any analysis of the character and history of the United States. More importantly, positive interaction between the races is essential to our progress, as noted by distinguished historian Felix Cohen: "The real epic of America is the yet unfinished story of the Americanization of the white man."[11] The integration of the best of both cultures is felt by many to have been in the 'higher plan' of things. It was hoped that the encounter between the technically capable, mentally-oriented Europeans and the spiritually and Earth reverent, heart-oriented Native Americans would bond these beneficial traits.

Astrologer and philosopher Dane Rudhyar theorized that the European white race was destined to develop technically in order to explore the world and establish a global network of society and communication. This unification of the world was an indispensable step in creating the emergence of a global consciousness. This evolutionary step in the consciousness of Homo Sapiens would then be followed by a leap into the new Aquarian Age of group consciousness and the Universal Brother/Sisterhood of Humankind. Rudhyar says the coming of Jesus Christ and his teachings gave the European race the opportunity to carry out their destiny as a mission of love and peace. If the Europeans had truly embraced Christ's message of love, then fulfilling their destiny would not have degenerated into a mission of war and genocide.

There are elements of Astrological karma and lessons evident in the U.S. birthchart which illustrate why we would fail to treat the Indians more humanely. These same elements indicate why our nation was split from birth into the divisions of North and South, which inevitably lead to the Civil War. Additional birthchart elements underscore the continuing conflict between our progressive vision and our conservative 'status quo' consciousness. These elements of potential conflict and tension will be examined in the next chapter.

1   *Astrology Plus*, Hilarion, pp. 11-12
2   Ibid. p. 21.
3   *America's Invisible Guidance*, Corinne Heline, p. 20.
4   *America's Assignment With Destiny*, Manly P. Hall, p. 110.
5   *The Eagle and the Shield*, R. Patterson and R. Dougall, p. 85.
6   This allusion was mentioned in the book *America's Secret Destiny*, by Robert Hieronimus Ph.D. Mr. Hieronimus has started a network of people interested in supporting legislative efforts to complete the Great Seal through the creation of a stamp of the Reverse of the Seal. Those interested in this work may write: Great Seal Network, 4801 Yellowwood Avenue, Baltimore, MD. 21209.

7   Forgotten Founders, Dr. Bruce E. Johansen, P. xiv. Found
         in *America's Secret Destiny*, Robert Hieronimus Ph.D., p. 8.
8   *The Importance of Gaining and Preserving the Friendship of
         the Indians to the British Interest Considered*, A. Kennedy,
         from James Parker, found in *America's Secret Destiny*, p.11.
9   *Indian Givers*, Jack Weatherford, pp. 121-122.
10   *Agrarian Justice*, Thomas Paine, p. 337. Found in *Indian
         Givers*, Jack Weatherford, p. 126.
11   Americanizing the White Man, Felix Cohen. Found in
         America's Secret Destiny, Robert Hieronimus Ph.D., p. 9.

3

TENSION AND CONFLICT WITHIN THE U.S. BIRTHCHART

Before I begin to look at the tensions within the U.S. birthchart, I would like to examine some of the additional positive factors brought to bear upon the U.S. in its birth and early life. One of these factors is the positive influence of the planets Venus, Jupiter, and the Sun, all in positive aspect to our Moon in Aquarius.

Let us first consider the influence of the Sun. In Chapter One I referred to the Sagittarian Ascendant of the U.S. as representing the self-image of the U.S. The Sun's placement in a birthchart, however, indicates the true nature of the soul or 'Higher Self' of the individual, as opposed to simply the self-image. The Sun in the U.S. birthchart is placed in the sign of Cancer. Hilarion says regarding the sign Cancer:

> The Cancer individual is one who, in a former incarnation, lived a life of devotion to the family unit, who nurtured and cared for others with great dedication,…the very act of serving the race in this way brings about, at the soul level, a deep tap into a very high source of nurturing impulses, and these are then available to be expressed at the personality level, filters permitting.

Hilarion adds that the main challenge for many individuals is to reconnect with the energies of their Sun sign. This is essential because the Sun is your soul essence, who you really are. It is, however, common for individuals to fail to fully express the true nature of their Sun sign. Other factors in the birthchart, such as the self-image of the Ascendant, or other placements, often serve as 'filters,' which may make it more difficult to own and express the innate qualities of our individual Sun sign. [1]

Applying these insights to the U.S. birthchart, we see that the true nature of the United States is the potential to manifest the caring qualities of Cancer, its Sun sign. The Cancerian caring, secure and embracing potential of the U.S. is well expressed by the Statue of Liberty, stationed to greet those arriving on our shores in search of a new home and security. The base of the Statue of Liberty proclaims:

> The New Colossus Not like the brazen giant of Greek fame, with conquering limbs astride from land to land; Here at our sea-washed, sunset gates shall stand a mighty woman with a torch whose flame is imprisoned lightning, and her name Mother of Exiles. From her beacon-hand glows world-wide welcome; her mild eyes command the air-bridged harbor that twin cities frame. "Keep ancient lands your storied pomp!" cries she with silent lips. "Give me your tired, your poor, Your huddled masses yearning to breathe free, The wretched refuse of your teeming shore. Send these, the homeless, tempest-tost to me, I lift my lamp beside the golden door!"
>
> Emma Lazarus (1849-1887)

The Sun, Jupiter, and Venus are all in the sign Cancer in our birthchart. They are also all 'conjunct' (placed closely to each other), as a group. In addition, as a group they are in 'trine,' or positive aspect, to the Aquarian Moon. The Moon represents the influences in childhood and early life. These three planets therefore contributed their particular energies to this area of our experience. Of the specific effect of Jupiter in Cancer Hilarion says:

> In Cancer, ruled by the Moon, Jupiter is in its exaltation. Inevitably with such a placement, the individual has received some definite benefit from the early home environment. This could be material, emotional, mental or just in terms of a positive self-image.[2]

And in relation to Venus in Cancer Hilarion says:

> Well-aspected, Venus here gives a very warm love-nature, and one that seeks to find its best expression within the context of the home environment.[3]

The characteristic energies of these three planets, when in positive relationship to the Aquarian Moon, were expressed in the deep emotional bonding the colonists experienced to their new lands in North America, and with each other as they fought the British to become free and sovereign over their own land.

Saturnian Conflict With Parental Authority

The planet Saturn has been an important and major influence upon the U.S. during our birth and throughout our nationhood. Saturn is the planet which represents where you must learn and grow through the experience of limitation and restriction. As previously mentioned, Saturn in positive aspect brings the qualities of commitment, loyalty, perseverance, and a willingness to 'hang in for the long haul'.

In the U.S. birthchart Saturn indicates conflict in childhood with 'authority,' due to its house placement and by its aspects. Saturn is located within the Tenth House, the house having to do with work, career, and role in the world. The Tenth is also one of two 'parental' houses in Astrology. The significance of having Saturn in the Tenth House is described by Hilarion:

> The tenth house is also a "parental house" and an afflicted Saturn in this position will tend to coincide with a strained relationship with one of the parents. [4]

The Saturn in our birthchart is, indeed, afflicted by a 'square' to the Sun. The tension of having Saturn square to the Sun is addressed by Hilarion:

> When Saturn is aspecting the *Sun*, there will always be a problem within the person in dealing with one of the parental figures. [5]

The theme of conflict with parental authority is attributable to Saturn's placement in the Tenth House and is accentuated by the difficult aspect of the square to the Sun. Such Saturnian tension with parental authority aptly describes our early relationship with Britain, especially our resentment of the laws and governing authority of the king. The royal Saturnian, parental authority was in 'square,' in tension with, the qualities of our Sun in Cancer. Someone born in the sign Cancer is very concerned with, and protective of, their own home. When King George III's laws seemed to arbitrarily restrict the colonists sense of home and security, they felt they had no choice but to fight back against that authority. As the Revolution escalated this tension also instigated the split between the 'Loyalists,' those remaining loyal to the Crown, and the freedom-seeking revolutionaries.

The antagonism of the early relationship between the U.S. and Britain illustrates the historical roots of this Saturnian tension in our birthchart. It also illuminates a pattern of Saturnian tension within the collective psyche of the U.S. This tension, represented symbolically here, has expressed itself in various ways at different times in our history.

Saturnian Limitation Vs. Jupiterian Optimism

The Saturnian tension is also involved in its relationship to Jupiter in our birthchart. Jupiter, being conjunct to the Sun, is therefore also 'squaring' Saturn. In positive aspect, Jupiter represents optimism, enthusiasm, faith, generosity, and beneficence. In difficult aspect, Jupiter represents exagerration, over-enthusiasm , 'biting off more than you can chew,' characteristics which we will review later in this chapter.

The tension of Saturn upon Jupiter's optimism is apparent in the conflict with our authoritative parent Great Britain. The Saturnian, traditional, conservative, authoritative force of Britain clashed with the Jupiterian optimism, faith, and enthusiasm of the colonists. Following U.S. independence the symbolic energies of this Saturn/Jupiter tension continued to manifest in conflict, commencing with the debate over what form of government we would establish for ourselves.

This debate peaked during George Washington's first term of office. The Saturnian force was personified by Alexander Hamilton, Washington's Secretary of the Treasury. The deeply conservative

Hamilton sought to impose a European/Old World, authoritative, even monarchical structure of government on our young nation. For example, Hamilton thought the Senate and the Presidency should be positions held for life. The Jupiterian force was personified by Thomas Jefferson, Washington's, Secretary of State. Jefferson enthusiastically advocated for a truly new idealistic, democratic order based on individual freedom. This conflict is well expressed in the words of Jefferson's biographer, James Schottler:

> Hamilton was for repressing popular tendencies and keeping Democracy restrained by the strong hand of order and authority: Jefferson was for giving Democracy the freest scope possible, and trusting willingly to the experiment of recognizing public opinion and the common sense as the ultimate repository of power. Hamilton believed in Statecraft, was dazzled by the example of the Caesars, desired a government whose strength lay in attaching wealth and privilege to its standard; while Jefferson considered that no government on earth could be so strong as that which offered its best advantages to everyone, and advanced its standard not so much by fostering as by giving equal opportunities...He [Hamilton] was for centralization, for imperialism for a strong national administration which would pervade every part of this Union...he [Jefferson] disdained corporate wealth, loved simple equality, simple manners, the open life, and dreaded every avenue which opened to bribery. In short, Hamilton was for re-erecting and re-enacting Europe in America; while Jefferson felt fervent faith that Heaven had reserved this hemisphere for a political destiny and experience of its own, through whose influence the Old World might, perhaps, in time become reorganized. Hamilton believed the free tendencies of mankind were essentially vicious, and needed domination; while Jefferson believed that human and individual domination had been, in the world's annals of the past, the fatal obstacle to public virtue.[6]

In regard to the opinions expressed above, we could say that the Saturnian 'parental,' authoritative influence in the U.S. birthchart represented not only Britain, but the whole European, Old World mentality.

The Civil War

The tension between Jupiterian idealism and Saturnian limitation was, as noted earlier, personified by Thomas Jefferson and Alexander Hamilton respectively in the battle over what form of government our nation would adopt. In Jefferson's Astrological birthchart, the Sun is in the 23rd degree of the sign Aries. This position of the Sun is opposite to the position of Saturn in the U.S. birth chart. Jefferson's battle with Saturnian, restricted, limited vision also appeared in his battle with Southern leaders over whether slavery would be allowed in our new nation. This was yet another conflict of Saturnian limitation with Jupiterian optimism and beneficence. We will explore how the seeds of this conflict, born of the Jupiter/Saturn tension, later ripened into our Civil War.

Jefferson made several statements against slavery in his political career. He attempted to include a statement outlawing slavery in the Declaration of Independence. This was rejected by the Southern states. Jefferson was compelled to compromise his ideals in exchange for Southern votes to create the Constitution and our democratic form of government. However, the gap between the North (Jupiter) and South (Saturn) continued to widen. Here is one of Jefferson's statements against slavery and one of his statements expressing fear for the future:

> I tremble for my country when I reflect that God is just. I can say with conscious truth that there is not a man on earth who would sacrifice more than I would to relieve us from this reproach in any practicable way. [7]

> ...unity of the nation could be broken when the hopes, institutions and culture of the two distinct geographical halves of the country were in opposition to one another...The ambiguous words of a paper Constitution would be scattered before the tempestuous winds of ambition, self-interest and passion untempered by understanding or love. [8]

Obviously, the enslavement of human individuals for economic benefit was in moral conflict with the idealism of a nation dedicated to 'life, liberty, and the pursuit of happiness'.

The Southern states would have liked to have divided the nation into a Saturnian/Southern portion, and a Jupiterian/Northern portion. The southern form of democracy likely would have followed the ancient Greek pattern of democracy, which permitted slavery. In contrast, the northern model of democracy likely would have remained new and incorporated Christian ideals of brotherly love and charity. It would have remained close to the truly free and equal form of democracy practiced by the Indians in the Iroquois League of Six Nations. The conflicts between the Greek and Indian political models have been aptly expressed by author Jack Weatherford in his book: *Indian Givers: How the Indians of the Americas Transformed the World*:

> Not all the founding Fathers showed interest in Indian political traditions. They turned instead toward models such as the British Parliament and some of the Greek and Italian city-states. [9]

> In the United States, the southerners identified much more closely with the ideals of Greek democracy based on massive slavery than with Iroquois democracy, which did not permit slavery. As historian Vernon Parrington wrote, the "dream of a Greek civilization based on black slavery was discovered in the bottom of the cup of southern romanticism". [10]

> Although the Greek cult spread out of the south, New Englanders never embraced it very fondly. For them mystic philosophies such as Transcendentalism, often accompanied by ideas of liberty and abolition of slavery, seemed far more alluring. For them the existence of slavery at the foundations of democracy bastardized the whole system. [11]

We can equate the Southern Greek acceptance of slavery as Saturnian, and the Northern 'mystic philosophies of transcendentalism' as Jupiterian.

At the moment that the first shots were fired at Fort Sumter, South Carolina, thus starting the Civil War on April 12, 1861, the Sun was at the 23rd degree of the sign Aries. As noted earlier, this was the exact same position that the Sun had occupied in the birthchart of Thomas

Jefferson. The Sun at that exact degree was, again, in opposition to the restrictive, limitation of Saturn in the birthchart of the U.S., as had the person and being of Jefferson when he was alive.

A significant planetary influence which helped ignite the Civil War was the transit of Uranus. This transit involved the planet Uranus, in the sky of 1861, 'conjuncting' (occupying the same position of) the placement of Uranus in the U.S. birthchart. It takes the planet Uranus 84 years to make one complete circle around the 360 degrees of the Zodiac. When one reaches the age of 84, one experiences a 'Uranus return,' the return of Uranus to the position which it occupied at the moment of one's birth. This event adds a new focusing of Uranian energy upon the effect of Uranus in one's birthchart. It would serve to renew and re-emphasize the Uranian energies of freedom, liberation, change. The United States turned 84 years old on April 12, 1861 when the Civil War began. 'Transiting' Uranus was exactly conjunct to the 'natal' Uranus in the U.S. birthchart, and was moving into an exact 'trine' with the natal Saturn in the birthchart over the next two years. In effect, the outbreak of the Civil War is the result of the second 'Uranian' revolution for the cause of freedom in our history.

Uranus rules the sign Aquarius. At the time of the eruption of national conflict during the Civil War, this nation was blessed to have as president someone who was born with his Sun in Aquarius, and with his Uranus in positive aspect to both Mercury and Jupiter. An Aquarian individual, again, according to Hilarion: "is one who, in a prior life, dedicated his energies to bringing others together into a united group and encouraging love and brotherhood between them". Someone who could keep the country united. A leader who would encourage "charity towards all, and malice towards none". That leader being, of course, President Abraham Lincoln.

Saturn And U.S. Acceptance Of Its Role In The World

In the U.S. birthchart Saturn is situated in the Tenth House, which is concerned with work, career, and role in the world. A powerful dynamic is revealed by Hilarion's comments on the lesson to be learned with having Saturn in the Tenth House:

> When Saturn is found in the tenth sector, the meaning is that the individual must put considerable effort into his job or career in order to make it a success. Lacking this effort — and a good deal of care and caution — the career will tend to turn sour again and again. The lesson is simply to devote a reasonable effort to making one's job a success. If this is done, them no problems will be encountered. However, past life habits of sloth and inattention have usually been brought forward into this life, and it is these which the job reverses are meant to correct.[12]

I am not sure if the U.S., as a collective entity, is carrying past life karma into this present life. However, I do see the symbolic significance and effect of this Saturn placement upon the character and experience of this country. My interpretation of this lesson for the U.S. is that we must make a sustained and disciplined effort to perform our vital role in the evolution of life on this planet. Hilarion clarifies that role: "In times past, the consciousness of the North American people clung to these traditions of liberty and equality with great tenacity, and through their steadfastness a wondrous ray of light from the Eternal was anchored into the land where these nations stand." These traditions of liberty and equality are exemplified by the Aquarian ideals of men like Thomas Jefferson and Thomas Paine, who envisioned America's experiment with democracy as our role in a grand order that would ultimately benefit the entire planet. In the words of Corinne Heline:

> Jefferson's wish was to widen rather than to narrow every policy. Like Thomas Paine, he looked beyond the welfare of his own country and embraced the future good of all men. He ever looked and worked for the time when man's interest would reach out beyond the local concerns and become truly universal.
>
> In a forward-looking monolith written during his Presidency he set forth some of his New Age concepts and voiced his faith in the time when man, in his steady upward progress, would

transcend his present limitations and enter into a larger and more inclusive human fellowship. He dreamed the true Aquarian dream of erased boundary lines, dissolved racial antipathies and world order in which the present rival armies and navies would be resolved into a single police force committed to maintaining universal peace. In all this he was in truth, projecting something more of the divine Plan for the eventual perfection of the human race.[13]

From these statements one can accept that the truly intended U.S. role in the world is to anchor a ray of light from the eternal, with the qualities of liberty and equality. However, Saturn in the Tenth House 'habits of sloth and inattention' have made it such that Saturn has continually limited and restricted our ability to fully accept and perform the positive role which Providence has set forth for us. U.S. efforts to promote and protect the ideals of liberty and equality have been irregular and often inadequate. The recurring cycle of 'isolationist' and 'protectionist' policies of this country demonstrate how Saturnian rings restrict our care and concern for those outside of our own borders. Fortunately, the clamp of Saturnian limitations have been loosened with sporadic bursts of 'Jupiterian' beneficence. The best example is how the U.S. finally entered into World War II, aggressively promoted the establishment of the United Nations, and launched the Marshall Plan to help Europe rebuild after that war. Unfortunately, the scale of our efforts has shrunk since then. I think it is fair to say that we have largely returned to a Saturnian, self-involved, laziness in relation to our role in the world. U.S. foreign aid has dropped, and even then 50 % of that aid is military aid and much of the rest related to U.S. corporate investments. In a poll it was revealed that most Americans think that we give too much Foreign Aid, however, when asked how much Aid would be enough, the amount specified was generally far less than what we actually give.

U.S. Resentment Of Authority

There is yet another distinctive Saturnian tension in the U.S. birthchart which would influence our experience of our role in the world. Saturn aspecting the Sun influences the way that we relate to any kind of authority. Regarding this specific influence Hilarion says:

> Saturn in aspect to either of the Lights [Sun or Moon] will bring into the life blockages in terms of dealing with authority, with government, with the police, or with any other authority-concept. The purpose of this pattern, both inside and out, is to bring the individual to the point of recognizing that there is value in guidelines, laws and restrictions — that man must play his "games" in accordance with rules, or else the games cannot exist. The failure to heed this lesson in past lives has led to loss and backsliding in terms of the learning of soul-lessons.[14]

This Saturnian 'blockage in terms of dealing with authority' is what leads the U.S. to resist any kind of external world authority, or even world opinion, towards its behavior. This resentment of authority is why we resist giving full support to the governing authority of the U.N. It is also why we refuse to give support to a World Legal Justice Court, which would have the power to bring indictments for criminal wrongdoing against any nation in the world, including the U.S. The power of this Saturn/Sun tension helps us understand why elements in the U.S. oppose such a court when it is supported by all of the other developed nations. This tension is reflected again in our refusal to sign on to world collective agreements regarding environmental regulations, such as the 1997 Kyoto treaty on global warming. The Saturnian tension that drives our authoritative, materially concerned, and manipulative actions will persist until we agree to play by the rules of the world community. This is yet another Saturnian, karmic component which limits our capacity to play the role and do the work which this nation was born to do.

Positive Planetary Influences

Pluto, that great bringer of change, has arrived to provide us a deeper insight into and transformation of, our Sagittarian self-image. At the same time, Pluto, by 'transit,' is 'sextiling,' making a positive aspect to our Saturn in the Tenth House. The Tenth House, again, is the house concerned with one's role in the world. We earlier examined how Saturn's placement in this house has restricted America's ability to perform its important role in the world. In carrying out our mission to advance liberty and equality in the world Hilarion warned that we need to make a considerable and sustained effort.

The Plutonian purpose behind this transit to our Tenth House Saturn along with the events of 9/11 is to allow us to look more deeply into our experience of our role in the world as well as to look deeply at how we see ourselves. We can explore all the ways in which our Saturnian isolationist, self-involved, material-mindedness has really limited our ability to know what is really going on in the world. Hopefully, by experiencing this Plutonian insight and transformation we can fully accept the responsibility to play the most positive and beneficent role in the world that we can. That is, at least, the potential of this positive 'transiting' Pluto aspect upon our Saturn.

An encouraging sign is the proliferation of media programs since the 9/11 events that are investigating the reality of the Arab world. Such research can help Americans understand what grievances serve as the basis for widespread Arab resentment of the U.S. Whether we will truly embrace the potential of this Plutonian insight, and thereby transform our resistance to accepting responsibility for our true role and mission in the world remains to be seen. These planetary influences, which come into effect via these transiting planets, provide the opportunity to learn important lessons. However, these influences are only in effect for a certain time period. It is up to us to take advantage of these opportunities while they are available.

Another positive planetary influence that can help the U.S. perform its role in the world is the positive aspect (a trine) between Uranus and

Saturn in the U.S. birthchart. I mentioned earlier that Uranus rules the sign Aquarius. It is the planet of freedom, revolution, and sudden unexpected change. I also mentioned how the physical, concrete reality of Uranus was discovered in 1781, months before the end of our Revolutionary War. This positive alignment contributes the Uranian energies of freedom and independence to help liberate our role in the world from the self-enclosed limitations imposed by Saturn in our Tenth House and Saturn square to the Sun. It was these Uranian energies which enabled the U.S. to liberate itself from the Saturnian, limiting, authoritative parent of Great Britain. It was this Uranian new ideal of freedom and individual equality erupting into conscious awareness for the first time in 1781 which kept the Saturnian, Hamiltonian forces from establishing a monarchical, authoritative, 'Old World' style of government in this country. As mentioned earlier, it was this Uranian influence upon our Saturn which was being stimulated by Uranus 'in the sky' conjuncting our natal Uranus and trining our natal Saturn. This was, again, a second revolution of liberation. A relevant question is: When will the next one occur?

Healing And Integration

The United States has two squares and one opposition within its Astrological birthchart. These tensions have and will manifest in many different ways as we evolve as a nation. The best way of healing the tension between any planets which are 'square' or 'opposite' to each other is to be able to embrace and integrate both realities. We have focused considerable attention on the negative attributes of Saturn. Jupiter in difficult aspect will produce qualities of exaggeration, over-enthusiasm, and 'biting off more than you can chew'. These traits were expressed in the Jupiterian zeal of Jefferson and Paine to create our innovative democracy. It is likely, however, that if Saturn's influence had not confronted this Jupiterian eagerness, then our founders would have bitten off more than they could chew by creating an idealistic, yet impractical, government. Fortunately, compromises were made resulting in the system of checks and balances we enjoy and which reflect the tension between Saturn and Jupiter. Astrologer Dane Rudhyar has pointed out how this was the very process involved in the framing of our governing Constitution:

The Constitution was built on many a compromise between the ideals formulated by the men of the Enlightenment and by Masonic and related groups, and the concrete realities of the day. Thus while Jefferson and especially Thomas Paine saw America as a great experiment in working out a "new order" of society that would eventually spread over the entire world, Washington, Hamilton, John Adams and many others were primarily concerned with building a nation, self-reliant and powerful among other nations.[15]

Of course one cannot pin the effect of any one course of action upon any one Astrological factor. There is always an amalgam of different factors influencing our collective consciousness and decisions. Examining all the individual factors, as I am trying to do now, can provide new levels of insight into why we do the things we do, what we need to learn from it, and how to improve. Only by admitting and understanding these tendencies can we Americans learn how to best pilot our nation.

In counseling an individual with these kinds of tensions, I would explain that it is the conflicts within us which force us to align our consciousness with what could be called our 'Higher Self' or Soul. It is only from this 'transpersonal' level of consciousness that you can embrace and integrate the seeming paradoxical dichotomies within you into a coherent, positively functioning whole. Otherwise, there is the tendency to simply project one end or another of the planetary qualities of these squares or oppositions onto somebody else. I tell my clients that insight into such conflicts can explain all of those personal relationships that you look back on later and say: "Why did I ever get involved with somebody like that?". These individuals appear in our lives to reflect to our conscious awareness the denied, unacknowledged parts of ourselves.

When looking at an entire nation in regard to these Astrological patterns of conflict, there is the likelihood that the nation itself will divide into different factions representative of the psychic tensions within the birthchart. These tensions have surfaced in the struggles between Jefferson and Hamilton, as well as the North and the South. In our present day society they have materialized as the clash between conservative and progressive elements. In the next chapter I will continue to look at sources of conflict and tension which exist within the U.S. birthchart. It is my hope that, by becoming more conscious of the sources of these tensions and the lessons involved, we can, as a nation, move to that 'transpersonal consciousness,' to the single eye above the pyramid, and fulfill the mission we were assigned to fulfill.

1   *Astrology Plus*, Hilarion, p. 6.
2   Ibid. p. 58
3   Ibid., p. 45.
4   Ibid., p. 147.
5   Ibid., p. 64.
6   Biography of Jefferson by James Schottler in 1897, found in *The Astrology of America's Destiny*, Dane Rudhyar, pp. 47-49.
7   Found in *America's Invisible Guidance*, Corinne Heline, p. 141.
8   Ibid., p. 140.
9   *Indian Givers: How the Indians of the Americas Transformed the World*, Jack Weatherford, p. 145
10 Ibid., p. 146
11 Ibid., p. 147.
12 *Astrology Plus*, Hilarion, p. 147.
13 *America's Invisible Guidance*, Corinne Heline, p. 58.
14 *Astrology Plus*, Hilarion, p. 64.
15 *The Astrology of America's Destiny*, Dane Rudhyar, p. 151.

4

CAUSES FOR MATERIAL SUCCESS AND OBSESSION IN THE U.S.

The United States is clearly the wealthiest nation which has ever existed in the known history of the Earth. This has been a great blessing for us. However, it can also be a curse. In the future, this affluence will be either the greatest blessing for ourselves and for what we can give to the world, or it will be a curse which will lead to our undoing.

Promises Of Success

There are two Astrological factors which relate specifically to our rise to riches. The first factor we shall examine is the positive 'trining' aspect between Uranus and Saturn in our birthchart. This factor becomes particularly significant because Uranus is situated in the Sixth House, the house related to the sign Virgo. The Sixth House is concerned with the experience of daily activity, of the mind engaged upon technical details, and the concept of service in the world.

As stated earlier, Uranus is the planet related to the qualities of freedom, independence, and sudden radical change. Additional qualities attributed to the influence of Uranus are intuition, originality of thinking, inventiveness, electricity and other forms of advanced technology, and mass communications. Having these Uranian qualities available in the Sixth House environment of mental application to technical details has produced in the U.S. a powerhouse of invention and technological innovation.

This Uranian innovative energy is in positive aspect to the planet Saturn in our birthchart. In positive aspect, Saturn is the planet of commitment, perseverance, responsibility, and concrete manifestation in the material world. Having these two planets in positive relationship to each other is why we possess not only the intuitive 'out of the loop' inventiveness of Uranus, but also the Saturnian capacity to manifest concretely functioning embodiments of those intuitive, innovative inventions. This explains why foreign inventors have often come to these shores to have their research supported and implemented into actual production. America's rise to unprecedented wealth has been fostered by the fortunate alliance of Saturnian substance with Uranian innovation in electricity, advanced technology, and communications.

There is another effect derived from a positive Saturn/Uranus aspect which would lead to our rise to riches. An individual who has a positive relationship between Saturn and Uranus within their natal birthchart is someone who has the ability to go 'between worlds'. Saturn and Uranus are planets that are normally difficult to integrate. Saturn represents the traditional status quo, while Uranus represents the non-traditional and unconventional. However, when these planets are in positive aspect to each other one discovers the ability to move freely between these opposing realms. This positive aspect also provides the ability to go between generations. Individuals with this Saturn/Uranus aspect can relate to people quite older as well as quite younger than themselves. Obviously, not all Americans necessarily exhibit these capacities, but they are common in our society.

The positive Saturn/Uranus aspect's ability to go between worlds and not be subjugated by either has allowed our society to reject the suffocation of European style 'class' society. This is especially the case as one considers the Saturn in the U.S. birthchart as representative of our 'parent' Great Britain. The liberating effect of Uranus in relationship to that rigid Saturnian parent would serve to emancipate us from the stratified and static social classes of our parent nation. This experience of liberation from old Saturnian class structure unleashed a spirit of entrepreneurial enthusiasm and spontaneity in the U.S. In contrast, Great Britain was born into the Astrological sign of Capricorn, which is ruled by Saturn. If there was ever a country which continues to struggle with the legacy of limiting definitions of class, it would be Great Britain.

The great gap between the British laboring class and the aristocracy was illustrated to me while visiting Britain. I was told the story of a man who came from a working class background. He had done quite well in business and found himself associating much more with the wealthier 'blue blood' classes of society. In Britain people can often tell from which class you come from by your accent. This man had done what many in his situation in Britain do. He took speech classes to change his working class accent. One day he was with a group of upper class gentlemen in a meeting and the servant lady came in to serve them tea. When she served this man his tea he slipped up for a moment and said 'ta' instead of saying "thank you" as a gentlemen would. 'Ta' is a distinctly working class way of saying thank you in Britain, and it immediately alerted the bluebloods that he was not really one of 'them'.

One may argue that the U.S. has its own social class structure. That is undeniably true. However, class distinctions based on hereditary lineage are limited to a few aristocratic enclaves on the East Coast. Many of our leaders (Lincoln, Carter, Clinton) have risen to the national stage without the privileges entitled to the elite. Freedom of the individual to chart their own course is affirmed by Hilarion's previous comment that the United States is the country of individual freedom. Individuals who incarnate here are those who have earned the right of individual freedom. Our exercise of such freedom has rewarded the U.S. in many ways and is a testament to the positive Saturn/Uranus aspect in our birth chart.

In conclusion, the positive Saturn-Uranus aspect has influenced the rapid creation of American wealth through the combination of Uranian innovation with Saturnian capacity for material level manifestation. In addition this same aspect has enabled us to go between these opposing worlds, liberating individuals and entrepreneurs from the rigid barriers of social class. Class in America is based on money rather than heredity. The reality of money brings into focus another major Astrological factor influencing our destiny to become the wealthiest nation on the earth. It is also the factor indicative as to why we may be the most materially obsessed nation on earth.

Pluto In The Second House

The presence of money in the American psyche is so powerful and so obvious on many levels that it must relate to a powerful and significant factor in the U.S. birthchart. It does. This factor concerns the Second House of the chart, related to the sign Taurus. This is the house traditionally associated with the experience of money and resources. Guess which planet the U.S. has in the Second House? Good guess if you said Pluto, the planet Hilarion described as the 'irresistible force, sweeping all before it'.

The placement of Pluto in this house of money and resources indicates the transformation of our experience of ourselves in relation to money and resources. This would occur, in one manner, through an incredible amassing of material wealth and power within a very short time-span. This placement would also concur with the powerful, insidious, secret, i.e. 'Plutonian' corruption and manipulation of power by the wealthy and privileged throughout the history of this country. It would also indicate the American population's obsession with money and wealth. 'Worshipping the almighty dollar' is a phrase I have only heard in the U.S. Greedy people exist around the world, but I have never heard of a collective expression of this human trait of greed being elevated to the level of worship in other nations. 'Worshipping the almighty British Pound?'. 'Worshipping the almighty French Franc?'. I think people in those countries would laugh at such an expression.

I have counseled clients from different countries who work in the corporate business world. I often hear stories of incredible cut-throat greed and competition in American business. I almost never hear such stories from other countries. Stories of the abuse of power and wealth have become part of our national fabric. Even though we may espouse equality, the world is aware of the deep-rooted greed in a nation where 5 per cent of the population takes home 50 per cent of the income.

When people learn that I have previously lived and worked in most of the different nations in Europe, they often ask me: "Where did you like it the most in Europe?". My first reply is always that I truly love and hate every country I have ever been to, including my own. I then tell them a certain joke. The emphasis I wish to make in sharing this joke is in relation to the two characteristics of the U.S. portrayed.

The joke is: What is the difference between Heaven and Hell?.

In Heaven:
The British are the police.
The French are the cooks.
The Americans make the computers.
The Russians are the chess players.
The Germans are the managers.
The Swiss are the bankers.
And the Italians are the lovers.
In Hell:
The British are the cooks.
The Germans are the police.
The Russians make the computers.
The French are the chess players.
The Americans are the bankers.
The Italian are the managers.
And the Swiss are the lovers.

So, in Heaven the Americans make the computers. This is easily relatable to the previously mentioned capacity we have to concretely manifest Uranian, technological innovation. However, in Hell, the Americans are the bankers? Ironically, it was a Swiss banker, the bankers in Heaven, who explained to me why this would be so. He said that in Switzerland the banks understand that their existence is based on trust. The individuals who entrust their money to a bank expect that their trust will be honored by the bank. Swiss banks are traditionally conservative and careful in their handling of depositor's money. In contrast, he said that it is well known that American banks often abuse the trust of their depositors in pursuit of profit. U.S. banks are driven to make increasingly risky investments to produce ever higher returns for their shareholders—not their depositors. He mentioned certain American banks by name which he personally knew were in very great trouble due to this kind of activity.

At the time of this writing, the scandal involving the Enron corporation is a large topic in the daily news. Enron is the largest bankruptcy in the history of the U.S. As mentioned earlier, it gave election campaign donations to 71 of 100 senators and yet despite paper profits of almost $2 billion between 1996-2000, it paid no corporate federal income taxes in 4 of the past 5 years. Moreover, Enron received a $278 million tax rebate in 2000.

In a newscast on the program 'All Things Considered' on National Public Radio, February 6, 2002, reporter Wade Goodwyn interviewed a securities firm manager, John Olson, who had many years of experience with Enron. He spoke of the emergence of an aggressive 'attack dog attitude' in their corporate culture. He stated that normally natural gas businesses grow at 2 percent a year, power companies at 3 percent a year. Enron, however, was trying to grow at a rate of 15 percent a year. This obsessive ambition is what forced them into making mistakes and into trying to hide the losses.

According to Olson: "The problem was that the culture soon overcame all of the normal checks and balances in the company. Instead of a company that was moving along at 10 miles an hour, the company moved at 50, 60, 70, 80 miles an hour at the end. And when they went off into bankruptcy, they went off at 80 miles an hour." [1]

In another account I learned that Enron spent $80,000 to create a whole floor of their building to serve as a fake company. It was to function as a display for stock analysts visiting from Wall Street to prove that there was a bona fide company there, with workers busy at their computer terminals, etc. Except it was all fake.

My question is, how could so many people be willingly participating in such fraud without the truth ever getting out? It seems to me to reflect this Plutonian obsessive material greed which has spawned so pervasively within our corporate culture.

When I am in Europe I will sometimes be involved in a conversation with individuals who work for corporations there. In these conversations all someone has to say is that their company is under American management and everyone knows instantly what that means. No explanation is necessary. What that means is a working environment where profit is all that matters. People do not. An environment where there is the likelihood of people being laid off even if that puts unfair stress on the other workers, so as to create greater profit or stock value.

And yet, this willingness to 'tighten the belt' and lay off workers to reduce expenses doesn't seem to apply to those in charge. A telling statistic I recently came across states that the average CEO in a Japanese corporation earns 16 times the wages of an average worker in that same corporation. An average CEO in a German corporation earns 22 times the wages of a worker in that corporation. A CEO in an American corporation makes 410 times the wages of the average worker. This is insane. No wonder they are willing to go to such obsessive measures to gain obsessive amounts of profit. They have to to validate that much plunder. It all, however, bears the mark of Pluto, Pluto in the house of money and finances.

Commentators have stated that the collapse of Enron and the picture of corporate corruption emerging from that collapse has shaken the environment in the U.S. almost as much as the events of 9/11. When former CEO Kenneth Lay was before a Senate investigating committee one Senator said: "Mr. Lay, I believe you bear a great deal of responsibility for shaking the confidence of us being able to export capitalism".

Reviewing the Enron debacle Professor Paul Krugman noted: "I'm someone who favors government intervention in some cases, but I'm generally a free marketeer. And I've always thought that what I think of as 'leftist morality plays,' in which the greedy people at the top take off and leave the poor innocent working class in the lurch were silly.

Things like that really don't happen. Well guess what, this [Enron] was just like it. This was like the scene out of the *Titanic*, where the people on the upper decks are jumping into the lifeboats and hurling the poor lower deck passengers to their deaths. It's got to shake up your view".

Author Marianne Williamson, in her book *The Healing of America*, addressed our national greed. She printed a letter which she first saw at a traveling exhibit of the Vietnam Wall. It illustrates this country's capacity for greed, in combination with our issues of power and security, and how they are acted out in a very confused and unfortunate manner.

On the Second of July, 1967, Alpha and Bravo companies of the First Battalion, Ninth Marines were on patrol just a few hundred meters south of the DMZ.

Bravo blundered into a well set ambush at the marketplace; soon, Alpha, too, was in the thick of it.

The enemy consisted of a regiment of the North Vietnamese Army supported by artillery, heavy mortars, rockets, anti-aircraft guns, and surface-to-air missiles.

Charlie and Delta companies were rushed to the field in support, but the outcome had been decided. The Marines were overwhelmingly outnumbered.

But worse than that, they were equipped with Colt M-16 rifles. Their M-14 rifles, which had proven so effective and reliable, were stored in warehouses, somewhere in the rear.

The M-16s would fire once or twice —maybe more—then jam. The extractor would rip the rim off the casing. Then the only way to clear the chamber and resume firing was to lock open the bolt, run a cleaning rod down the barrel, and knock the casing loose. Soon it would jam again.

This was the rifle supplied to her troops by the richest nation on earth.

The enemy was not so encumbered. They carried rifles which were designed in the Soviet Union and manufactured in one of the poorest nations on earth — the so-called People's Republic of China. *Their* rifles fired. Fired every time. They ran amongst the Marines, firing at will.

Sixty-four men in Bravo were killed that afternoon. Altogether, the battalion lost around a hundred of the Nation's finest men. The next morning, we bagged them like groceries. We consigned their bodies to their families and commended their souls to God. May He be as merciful as they were courageous.

Today, people are still debating the issue: Was it the fault of the ammo? The fault of the rifle? Neither. It was the fault of the politicians and contractors and generals. People in high places knew the rifles and ammo wouldn't work together. The military didn't want to buy the rifle when Armalite was manufacturing it. But when Colt was licensed as the manufacturer, they suddenly discovered it was a marvelous example of Yankee ingenuity.

Sgt. Brown told them it was garbage. Col. Hackworth told them it was garbage. And every real Grunt knew it was garbage. It was unsuited for combat.

There was no congressional investigation. No contractor was ever fined for supplying defective material. No one uncovered the bribes paid to government officials. No one went to jail. And the mothers of dead Marines were never told that their sons went into combat unarmed.

To all outward appearances, those Marines died of gunshot and fragmentation wounds. But a closer examination reveals that they were first stabbed in the back by their countrymen.

The politicians, contractors, and generals have retired to comfortable estates now. Their ranks have been filled by their clones — greedy invertebrates every one. They should hope that God is more forgiving than I.

Brave men should never be commanded by cowards

First Lieutenant Harvey G. Wysong

0100308
United States Marine Corps Reserve
First Battalion, Ninth Marines

This kind of greed, which would knowingly be complicit in the death of innocent men, is hard to imagine. The placement of Pluto in this house of money and material gain indicates an area of major intensity and needed growth and transformation in the American experience. To again quote Hilarion regarding the effects of Pluto:

> The planet Pluto in astrology pertains to that which brings changes into the life — changes in attitude, changes in outlook, changes in the approach to certain areas. The changes indicated by Pluto in the chart are unavoidable and can be absolutely counted on to take place. In the case of most individuals, the changes come about "by force", i.e. they are resisted by the individual and must be rammed home by the implacable and irresistible force of events. When resistance is shown to such changes, the experiences are inevitably harder and more painful than they would have been if the individual had "seen the writing on the wall" as it were, and had voluntarily stepped in the direction in which the events were trying to move him.
>
> The position of Pluto *by house* is by far the most important of the indicators where this planet is concerned. [2]

Hilarion has commented on the Second House, but he doesn't specifically address Pluto in the Second House. The Pluto in the U.S. birthchart is experiencing both positive and difficult aspects. The positive aspect would bring in great material affluence, as Astrologer Alan Oken states: 'When it is well-aspected, Pluto in this position [the Second House] can act as a "never-ending fountain of gold."[3] Those are an interesting choice of words, recalling the discovery of the 'fountain of gold' in the western states during the Gold Rush.

The difficult aspect to Pluto however, would bring in karmic lessons and challenges in relation to wealth, money, and resources. Alan Oken explains: 'But when it is afflicted, it [Pluto in the Second House], can suddenly withdraw rewards worked for over a long period of time.'[4]

The Great Depression is an example of such Astrological forces at work. This is something I will examine later in the chapter. The difficult aspect to Pluto would also aggravate fears and insecurities over these issues of wealth, money, and resources. Authors Bruno and Louise Huber point out:

> The 2nd house corresponds to Taurus, a fixed earth sign. Insecurities in the areas of possession, wealth or self-worth can hinder personal development. Difficult planetary positions in the 2nd house suggest a fear about holding onto one's possessions, about securing oneself against possible interferences (often without real reason); about defending and insuring oneself in every way possible. It is the house wherein we build "castles" for protection and defense.

> Self-worth and self-defense are the two key words for the correct and incorrect functions of this house. If a human being is forced into self-defense and has strong tensions in the 2nd house, he will build around himself a wall that cannot be penetrated. He encapsulates himself in his own "I" (shell), goes into a "porcupine readiness", and considers other people as enemies, this can go to the extreme of paranoia.[5]

The concept of encapsulating oneself within a wall of protection explains why we Americans seek to shield ourselves by purchasing far more insurance than citizens of any other nation. It also explains why the U.S. periodically retreats into political 'isolationism' and 'protectionism,' and underscores our desire for a 'missile defense shield' to protect us from our enemies.

The lessons in the U.S. birthchart related to money, security, and self-worth are exacerbated by the fact that this Second House Pluto is in 'opposition' to, or in tension with, the planet Mercury. This is important because Mercury and Mars in Gemini are the two placements in the U.S. birthchart which relate specifically to the mental thinking and communicative experience of the U.S. These placements influence how well we comprehend our karmic lessons and how well we communicate our responses to them. We previously discussed how the placement of Mars in Gemini provided mental energy, intelligence, and clarity in the launching of our nation.

In contrast, the placement of Mercury in our birthchart is in the sign Cancer. Cancer is an emotional, water sign. For this position of Mercury Hilarion says:

> Mercury here if afflicted [which it is], will make it very difficult for the rational mental processes to operate independently of and unaffected by the emotional life. Negative feelings and emotions will have a way of muddying up the reasoning ability. The main lesson is to *separate thought from emotional influences*.[6]

The influence of this Mercury in opposition to Pluto in our second house is one reason why we can't seem to 'get it'. This 'muddied up reasoning ability' is what I would call *'fuzzy thinking'*. It explains why we can be a nation obsessed with dieting and losing weight while being generally oblivious to the hunger and starvation which exists both outside and inside our own borders. This confused, blurred Mercury, in opposition to our Plutonian karma relative to money and wealth, also explains why we cannot intelligently perceive and implement a coherent plan which would alleviate the suffering and moral compromise created by the disparity between our wealth and that of the rest of the underdeveloped world. This 'fuzzy thinking' also 'explains' why the characters who orchestrated the craziness at Enron thought they could get away with the incoherent ways that they tried to cover-up their excesses.

In Astrology there are numerous ways and levels at which the energies symbolized in an aspect such as this Pluto/Mercury opposition will tend to play out. In the last chapter I discussed how the tension between the planets Saturn and Jupiter in the U.S. birthchart could manifest in divisions within the U.S. population. The same phenomena could also occur here in relation to this Pluto/Mercury opposition. Powerful, wealthy, Plutonian corporations and other entities of media and political power, with their Madison Avenue advertising, political slogans, and 'sound bite' scraps of information, are mentally blurring the thinking capacity of the masses, i.e. Mercury in Cancer, 'muddied up thinking'. Marianne Williamson has accurately described this kind of mental unclarity:

> The average European is much better educated, much more aware of the true political and social issues that affect his or her daily life, than is the average American. We have become so accustomed to allowing the media to do our thinking for us that we are dangerously ignorant of important issues.[7]

> Without the strength of an enlivened mind we become passive observers to our own lives, easy to sell to and easy to control. Thus the onset of citizen anemia…We know more about fashion at the Oscars than we know about issues that vitally affect our daily lives. If this continues, democracy will become a memory.[8]

> We have so dumbed down the entire culture that anything that doesn't fit into the white bread section of the supermarket is deemed way too controversial for America to handle.[9]

This Mercury opposite Pluto tension will also resonate with the conflict and stress present in other difficult aspects in the U.S. birthchart. For example, we examined earlier the squaring of Saturn with Jupiter, whose resulting tension marked the conflict and moral compromises inherent in our accommodation of slavery. The conflict engendered by this difficult aspect was aggravated by the 'fuzzy thinking' resulting from this Mercury/Pluto tension. Both the North and the South were gripped by a distorted fear of the material and economic consequences of an abandonment of slavery. The Southern 'fuzzy thinking' is demonstrated by their living with a sense of upright moral rectitude, while allowing the enslavement of another race of human beings. The Northern 'fuzzy thinking' is exhibited in their belief that limiting the expansion of slavery into the new western states was adequate fulfillment of their moral obligations. Meanwhile, in a Pluto-like underworld, thousands of humans were suffering all the humiliations of slavery.

The 'fuzzy thinking' generated from the Mercury/Pluto tension also condoned the decimation of the Native American populations without much concern at all. This same tension also perverts the karmic lessons of wealth, money, and resources we earlier addressed in the difficulties rising from the placement of Pluto in the Second House. As a result we have continually sought to placate our fears with material greed and our insecurities with increased defense budgets.

A psychological analysis of some of the major neuroses within this country is provided by Astrologer Howard Sasportas' observations of Pluto in the Second House:

> With Pluto here it is necessary to discover the underlying motivations which propel such strong and passionate feelings about money and security. For some, money is imbued with the power of a deity, which determines if they live or die. Money and power may be accrued as a way of controlling others... Material success may be sought as a way of enhancing their sexual attractiveness. Some may see amassing possessions as a way of extending their territory of influence and thereby regaining a sense of their lost infantile omnipotence. Or if they have been put down and belittled as children, then acquiring great wealth and status may be the way of proving their worth to the world.
>
> Pluto sets up his altar of destruction in whatever house he occupies. Consequently, those with this placement may harbour a fear that something lurks in the shadows which threatens to wipe out their resources and possessions.... Pluto brings extremes, and they might experience both ends of the scale of poverty and wealth. If they have become too centred or identified with their bank accounts, cars or big homes, Pluto may destroy these external forms of self-definition, stripping away outer attachments or trappings so that they can discover who they are from inside themselves. They may even unconsciously provoke such a catastrophe so that an inner and more permanent sense of worth and security can be found.[10]

The key lesson here for Americans is to find that 'inner and more permanent sense of worth and security'. This is a major collective and karmic lesson for America. The above mentioned issues relating to sexuality and the life and death struggle are even more relevant when we look at the tension which this Second House Pluto is experiencing within the birthchart. As mentioned earlier, Pluto is in 'opposition,' in tension with, the planet Mercury. What has not been mentioned is that this Mercury is also placed in the Eighth House. The Eighth House is related to the Astrological sign Scorpio and its issues of sex, birth, and death. The repetition of these issues in our birthchart clarifies why issues of sex, death, and money often get tied-up in much of the American experience. In the next chapter I will look at how this Pluto/Mercury opposition affects the American experience of sexuality.

The Great Depression

Our relationship to money and wealth is a prominent theme in the U.S. birthchart. We have looked at several Astrological factors and their corresponding influences, such as our periodic retreat into isolationism to vainly try to protect our possessions. During the Great Depression (1929-1940), additional Astrological factors appeared in the transits of Saturn and Pluto. We will examine them to see why they indelibly impacted the way Americans view money, finances, and government.

The Great Depression has been largely associated with 'Black Tuesday,' the Stock Market crash on October 29, 1929. However, recent commentators have referred to that event as more like "a fatal heart attack for a patient also suffering from terminal cancer".[11] After World War I the nation had returned to its pre-war isolationism. It withdrew support for Woodrow Wilson's 'League of Nations,' ignoring his prophetic words: "The recent war ended our isolation. You have the alternative of armed isolation or peaceful partnership".

During the roaring 20's the economy and culture exploded with new optimism and affluence. On Wall Street people were making fortunes investing into new companies. People were pouring their life savings into stocks and securities. Banks were lending money left and right to new business ventures. However, there was an underground darkness stirring beneath all of the glitter. Farmers were suffering because prices for their crops collapsed after the war. There was large scale unemployment because of increased mechanization in factories, putting laborers out of work. Economic difficulties spread around the world because the rapid production of goods outstripped the demand.

Most of the wealth in the 1920's Stock Market existed only on paper. Government regulation was minimal and questionable trading practices flourished. To buy stocks on margin (credit), you didn't have to put up all of the money right away. You only had to pay 10-20% up front, and the rest on margin (credit). When foreign investors started to sell their stocks, investors here were asked to put up the cash they owed for their stocks. To come up with the cash, they had to quickly sell off some of their stocks. Here is where the panic started. Between late October and Mid-November, 1929, 40% of the value of the Market had vanished, a total of $30 billion lost in less than a month. 1,300 banks failed in one year. 5,000 banks failed over a 3 year period. The Depression was called the 'Great Depression' not only because of the loss of wealth, but because it lasted more than a decade.

Now, let us look at this Astrologically. Starting in December, 1927, until February, 1931, transiting Saturn, in the sky, had moved across the Sagittarian Ascendant, across the self-image of the United States. Saturn makes things 'real,' but it does it through heaviness, weight, and limitation. Saturn is kind of a 'reality-check,' forcing one to get 'real,' and align oneself with such Saturnian qualities as responsibility. This Saturn 'transit' forced the Sagittarian optimism of the nation to 'sober up' as the Depression deepened. In February of 1931, Saturn moved into the Second House of the U.S. birthchart, the house of money and finances. 1932 was when the country hit bottom and has been called the worst year of the Depression. In February of 1932, there was an exact conjunction of Saturn to the natal, Second House Pluto in the U.S. birthchart. This would symbolize a time of 'getting real' with our karma around wealth and money. Meanwhile, transiting Pluto, in the sky, had moved into an exact opposition to the transiting Saturn also in the sky. The tension between concrete, Saturnian reality, and a deeper, unavoidable, fated, Pluto destiny explains why the Depression affected people all around the world. The response in Germany to this Saturn/Pluto pressure was the rise to power of Adolf Hitler.

Returning to the U.S. experience, it takes the planet Pluto 247 years to go all the way around the 360 degrees of the zodiac. In the 1930's Pluto finally moved into exact opposition with its placement in the Second House. The position Pluto had occupied at our nation's birth in 1776. This Pluto transit, making an opposition to our 'natal' Pluto in our birthchart, was the source of the deep, unavoidable, on-going desperation, and also explains why the depression in this country lasted so long, truly testing men's faith, and made it the 'Great Depression'.

The deep impact of this Pluto transit transformed many aspects of the way that we relate to money, finance and government in this country. It undermined President Herbert Hoover's administration, which minimized the suffering of the Depression and instead continued to espouse the ethic of the 'rugged individualism of the self-made man'. The gravity of one third of America being out of work opened the way for President Roosevelt's 'New Deal' in 1932. The desperate times galvanized Americans into accepting that the collective will of the people, i.e. the government, can play a role in regulating aspects of business. As a result, Roosevelt created the modern Securities and Exchange Commission and installed the brilliant William O. Douglas to oversee the Stock Market. More importantly, Americans from now on would count upon their government to come to the aid of those who suffer misfortune in this society. One could sense that this material, financial, Plutonian 'ego-death' was necessary before the next big expansion of material, military, and political power which was to occur in the 1940's and 50's.

Neptune In Positive Aspect

The fortunate element in the U.S. Astrological karmic blueprint is that every planet in the birthchart which is experiencing a tense aspect with another planet is also experiencing a very positive aspect with some other planet. In essence, there is always somewhere else where the 'tensed' planet can 'go' for positive help and insight. In the case of the Pluto/Mercury opposition and its greed and fuzzy thinking, the positive relationship available is with the planet Neptune. Neptune is positively aspecting Pluto by 'trine,' and Mercury by 'sextile'. Neptune can, in essence, potentially heal and integrate both ends of this Pluto/Mercury tension. It can heal the greed, the fear, the insecurity, and all of the 'fuzzy thinking'. It can heal everything I have said so far about this Pluto, and this Mercury, and of the tensions between them.

The planet Neptune, in positive aspect, creates the capacity for spiritual faith and surrender, for compassionate sensitivity and empathy, and for unconditional love. It is the national experience of compassion for all of the innocent victims of the greed and duplicity at Enron which is finally stirring the conscience of the nation, resulting in passage of a new campaign finance law, and perhaps other measures as well.

The Neptune in the U.S. birthchart is in the Ninth House, the house of philosophy, religion, and your 'belief' system. Neptune placed here gives us a capacity to open to a true spiritual faith and knowledge. It is to this Neptunian spiritual faith and knowledge that we Americans need to turn to address our Plutonian, manipulative greed and Mercurial 'fuzzy thinking'. For example, if our incredible accumulation of wealth relative to the rest of the world was put in service to a Neptunian compassion for those who suffer needlessly on this planet what a different world this would be. Maybe this is why mystical symbols and the words 'In God We Trust' have been printed on our money, as a hidden reminder. I would say that Neptune in our birthchart is why, when we need it most, someone or something embodying a spiritual force appears to turn us in the right direction.

Divine guidance has been present in our affairs since the birth of the U.S. After days of argument over the creation of the new Constitution during the Continental Congress, when the members were about to abandon the effort, Benjamin Franklin said:

The small progress we have made after these weeks of continual reasoning with each other, our different sentiment on almost every question, is melancholy proof of the imperfection of the human understanding…In this situation of the assembly, groping to find political truth…let us apply to the Father of Lights to illuminate our understanding…God governs in the affairs of men. If a sparrow falls not to the ground without His notice, is it probable that an empire can arise without His aid? We have been assured in the sacred writings, that except the Lord build the house, they labor in vain that build it. I firmly believe this and also that without His concurring aid we shall succeed in this political building no better than the builders of Babel. We shall be divided by our little partial, local interests. Out project will be confounded and we ourselves shall become a reproach and a byword down to future ages. And what is worse, mankind may hereafter, from this unfortunate instance despair of establishing government by human wisdom and leave it to chance, war and conquest.

I beg leave to move that hereafter prayers imploring the assistance of Heaven and its blessings on our deliberations be held in this assembly every morning and that the clergy of this city be requested to officiate. [12]

In the dark days of the Civil War, Abraham Lincoln was also able to find support from divine guidance. As he said to a friend during the conflict:

I see the duty devolving upon me. I have read upon my knees the story of Gethsemane where the Son of God prayed in vain that the cup of bitterness might pass from Him. I am in the garden of Gethsemane now and my cup of bitterness is full and overflowing.

That the Almighty does make use of human agencies and directly intervenes in human affairs is one of the bible's plainest statements. I have had so many evidences of this direction, so many instances when I have been controlled by some other power than my own will, that I cannot doubt that this power comes from God. I frequently see my way clear to a decision when I am conscious that I have no sufficient facts upon which to found it. But I cannot recall one instance in which I have followed my own judgment, founded upon such a decision, where the results were unsatisfactory; whereas, in almost every instance where I have yielded to the views of others, I have had occasion to regret it.[13]

The divine guidance discussed by Lincoln and Franklin also appeared in the desperate times of the Great Depression. At the same time that 'transiting' Pluto was in opposition to our 'natal' Pluto in our birthchart during the Great Depression, Pluto was also 'sextiling' or making a positive aspect, to our 'natal' Neptune. We began to throw off the selfish greed of the 1920's and re-connect to the need for compassion for those who suffer. It was time to go beyond the 'rugged individualism of the self-made man' and we embraced the social conscience of F.D.R.'s 'New Deal'. It was also at this time that the reverse side of the Great Seal, with the divine eye of spiritual vision completing the man-made structure of the pyramid, first appeared to the American public on our dollar bills.

The True Meaning Of The Second House

The Second House is related to the Astrological sign Taurus and its concerns of money and material security. Hilarion gives some unique insight into the significance of the sign Taurus:

> The Taurus individual has, at the soul level, a deep understanding of the meaning of love. This is attested to by the rulership of Venus over this sign. The grasp of the right approach to love and its true meaning is again a gift which the soul has given itself — in this case, as a result of an incarnation in which a self-sacrificing love was cherished for another, usually without being fully returned. This act of selfless devotion allows the soul to tap deeply into a wellspring of pure love at a very high spiritual plane, which constantly feeds into the soul a great capacity for love and affection. Again, along with the gift comes a responsibility. In the case of Taurus, the task is to learn to express the love side unconditionally, simply allowing the

affection to flow into and through the personality without damming it up, and without attaching conditions to the giving of affection. If there is any damming up or restriction of the affectional impulses, a problem arises due to the desire of this abundance of love to find a suitable object. Denied an external object, i.e. another person, the love will usually lavish itself upon the individual's own physical body with its senses the primary focus. It is from this process that the oft-quoted tendency for self-indulgence in the Taurus stems. Another difficulty can also arise if the nature of suppressive habits in the Taurus individual are such as to prevent the thwarted affectional urges from expressing through self-indulgence. In such instances, it is possible for the love to center not on another individual but on possessions or money. This can occur when in the early childhood there was little physical affection shown by the parents. Thus, in the case of Taurus, the task at the personality level is to express love, without allowing the affectional urges to manifest as self-indulgence or an over-stressing of money or possessions.[14]

Many Astrological sources will note this tendency for Taurus individuals to be overly concerned with material security and money, or to exhibit a tendency towards sensual indulgence. However, only Hilarion provides this unique insight as to the inner cause of that material obsession or sensual indulgence. It is simply a force of love which, when it cannot go out and be expressed, is trying to return back in. The U.S. having its Pluto in this Taurean Second House indicates that the United States has the potential for either incredible love or incredible self-indulgence and greed. One cannot serve two masters. It will either be God or Mammon.

1   *All Things Considered*, National Public Radio, February 6, 2002

2   *Astrology Plus*, Hilarion, p. 77.

3   *Alan Oken's Complete Astrology*, Alan Oken, p. 334.

4   Ibid., p. 334.

5   *The Astrological Houses:A Psychological View of Man & His World*, Bruno & Louise Huber, p. 75.

6   *Astrology Plus*, Hilarion, p. 39.

7   *The Healing of America*, Marianne Williamson., p. 181.

8   Ibid. p. 182.

9   Ibid. p. 232.

10 *The Twelve Houses*, Howard Sasportas, pp. 314-315.

11 *Don't Know Much About History: Everything You Need to Know About American History but Never Learned*, Kenneth C. Davis,. Many of the facts recounted here were found in this book.

12 Found in *America's Invisible Guidance*, Corinne Heline, p. 74,

13 Also found in *America's Invisible Guidance*, Corinne Heline, pp. 133-134

5

America and Sex, Birth, Death

The American experience of the planet of complete transformation, Pluto, is in the Second House, the house related symbolically to the sign Taurus. In the last chapter, I quoted Hilarion's comments regarding the sign Taurus. In those comments, Hilarion stated that a Taurean individual could move towards physical self-indulgence as a form of compensation for a lack of opportunity to express love in their lives. Having our Pluto in the Second House indicates that we may have some deep lessons and needed transformation in relation to sexuality, wealth, and money. The theme of sexuality is accentuated by the fact that our Pluto is 'opposite,' in tense aspect to, Mercury in the Eighth House. The Eighth House is the house related to the Astrological sign Scorpio and its themes of sex, birth, and death.

Abortion

There are various aspects of the American experience which relate to these Scorpionic themes. There is one issue which clearly incorporates all three of these components: sex, birth and death. This is an issue which seems to be a much larger and more conflictive issue here in the U.S. than anywhere else in the world. This is the issue of abortion.

The way in which we Americans experience the issue of abortion reflects all of the qualities of the intense Mercury opposite Pluto tension in our birthchart. This includes the Mercury in Cancer quality of 'feelings and emotions muddying up the reasoning ability,' i.e. 'fuzzy thinking' which was explained earlier. I see 'fuzzy thinking' around this deep Plutonian, life and death power and control issue exhibited on both sides of the debate. The clearest comments which I have heard on the issue of abortion have been made by Hilarion. The books *Answers* and *More Answers* present compilations of answers given by Hilarion in response to a wide range of questions. This is Hilarion's reply to the question: "What is the karmic significance of abortion to the mother, the father and the foetus?"

The karmic significance depends, to a great degree, on the motives and reasons behind the action which terminates the life of the foetus.

Birth into earth incarnation is viewed on higher planes as a great opportunity for soul-advancement, for learning, and for spiritual progress. It is also seen by prospective souls as a chance to rejoin loved ones, and to participate in the fullness of physical existence on one of the most beautiful planetary oases in the universe.

Thus from the point of view of the soul that might have come into the world in the aborted foetus, the abortion is merely the shutting of a door, the loss of an opportunity to advance. However, as a general rule, souls who lose the possibility of earth incarnation through deliberate abortion are given another opportunity to incarnate very soon thereafter.

For the woman who arranges or assents to an abortion, the pivotal question is motive. If it is done for strictly selfish reasons, especially when the woman was in a situation in which the child could have been welcomed and cared for, then the killing of the foetus is counted as an act close to murder in the scale of seriousness. The karmic burden arising in such a circumstance is normally met and set aside through the experience of being denied a child when one is wanted...either later in the same life, or in some subsequent experience on the earth plane.

At the other end of the scale of motive is the situation in which there are persuasive reasons for terminating the pregnancy, reasons not related to simple selfish desires. For example, where there is a threat to the mother's life or health, or where no family situation exists capable of providing a good early life to the child, then abortion is not taken to be a particularly negative act. *Some* karma stems from it, of course, but it is generally not of a severe nature.

The father of the aborted child is also assessed in strict accordance with his motive, assuming he forces or persuades the mother to have an abortion.[1]

In light of the above explanation I feel that both sides of the debate are lacking true spiritual compassion and empathy. The 'Right to Lifers' lack compassion for the individual conditions and motives of the mother, as well as her right to determine for herself what is or isn't justified. The 'Pro-Choicers' lack, in some quarters, a sensitivity and acknowledgement of the seriousness of the karmic reality arising from terminating the life of an unborn child.

So, is abortion right or wrong? Without 'feelings and emotions muddying up the reasoning ability,' one would have to say that the issue cannot be framed in such black or white terms. It depends totally upon the motives of the persons involved. This Mercurial, mental/verbal debate has intense Plutonian overtones, as displayed in the bombings of abortion clinics, murdered doctors, and grisly photos of dead fetuses as well as dead mothers victimized by botched illegal abortions. There needs to be the introduction of the only thing which could heal this tension. The only thing which can approach this subject with true human compassion and empathy. Compassion and empathy for both the mother and the foetus. Not simply one or the other. This would be available if the Mercury, and the Pluto ends of this opposition could open to the positive 'trine' and 'sextile' aspects leading them to: Neptune. By embracing compassion and unconditional love, we can experience spiritual faith, trust, and surrender for both the mother and the child.

The Eighth House

Now that I have opened a Pandora's box of hot topics, we might as well go onto other controversial Eighth House issues. Many planetary placements in the Eighth House have to do with karmic lessons specifically related to sexuality. Mercury in the Eighth House is one of those planets. Hilarion has said that the experience of sexuality is one of the greatest gifts which the Creator has given us. Moreover, the way in which we experience sexuality now is nothing compared to the ways in which we will experience sex in the coming New Age. In my professional experience, nearly 75% of incarnating souls have indicators in their Astrological birthcharts showing a tendency in previous lives to over-emphasize the physical aspect of love. Previous lives where love has been made to be the servant of sex, rather than sex being the servant of love. Through the specific Astrological indicators involved, one can see a variety of ways in which these tendencies are to be rectified. One of those indicators is Mercury in the Eighth House:

In the eighth house, Mercury points clearly to a sexual emphasis. This planet, as we have already said, is both male and female. In the eighth, this hermaphrodite indicator points to a deep-lying confusion in terms of the sexual roles. In a typical case, the native was in recent lives of the other sex, and had strong sexual compulsions. In the present life, now in a different sexual body, these sexual drives try to express, but produce less than complete fulfillment. The soul simply has not learned to express its sexuality in the new form, and still expects the same rewards and sensations which were known in the previous incarnations. Almost invariably, the change in sexual identity was undertaken by the soul as a means of undercutting what it saw as a drift toward indulging in sexual experience for its own sake, i.e. with little or no affection being felt. Since this is one of the major gateways to the downward spiral, the soul has decided to cut short that process by changing sex. Always, of course, there is a risk that the new personality, even though of different sex, may still develop a habit of sexual indulgence without love being felt; however, the likelihood of this is greatly reduced. It normally occurs that the feelings of sexual frustration felt by the new personality are interpreted by him as arising because sex for its own sake is incomplete. That is just the conclusion that the soul is hoping for, because it may impel the conscious personality to re-examine his approach to sex, and to decide that sex without love is an empty experience.

Indeed, such a person will invariably find that, by allowing his sexual drives to express only with someone for whom genuine affection is felt, the feelings of frustration disappear.[2]

Homosexuality

Now, I don't think that this means that everyone in this country has recently changed gender from that which they were experiencing in previous lives. There are, however, many ways in which the significance of this placement is applicable to the American experience. First of all, another very explosive American issue is homosexuality. This is another area where I am, again, grateful to Hilarion for his clear insight, wisdom and knowledge. In most cases where an individual is drawn to a homosexual lifestyle, says Hilarion, it is simply a situation where that soul has been previously incarnating in a particular gender. It has then been seen that it would be useful for that soul to incarnate in the opposite gender, knowing that the soul may find it difficult to adapt to the opposite sexual expression. If it becomes too difficult to adapt, such souls may simply seek physical and emotional nurturing among their own sex. Hilarion emphasizes that 'In the eyes of the Creator, it has never been a sin,' to be homosexual.

It is clear to me in most cases that a gay man is largely a woman caught in a man's body, and that a gay woman is largely a man caught in a woman's body. There has always been a certain percentage of homosexuals in all cultures at all times. In Native American societies (where it is unlikely to find accusations of homosexuals being "mama's boys"), homosexuals were accepted and even acknowledged as having a special 'medicine'.

The American experience of homosexuality, however, has been intense and Plutonian. We have witnessed incredible suppression, draconian laws, and gay bashing on one hand, and gay pride, activism, and the intensity of the AIDS epidemic on the other hand. The AIDS epidemic exists in other nations as well, either in much smaller and less overt homosexual populations, or in Africa and Asia, where AIDS is more a heterosexual disease.

In earlier times, the dominant heterosexual culture held the Plutonian power and control. The American Psychiatric organization listed homosexuality as a psychological disease. Many states had 'anti-sodomy' laws on their books. This Plutonian power extended to material and financial control. Homosexuals were barred from many forms of employment. Facing such Plutonian control and power, the Mercurial, communicative 'voice' of the homosexual population was, seemingly, powerless. Many homosexuals were forced to hide the depth of their true being. They had to conceal their sexuality in 'the closet'.

As we have learned, Neptune is positively aspecting both ends of the Pluto/Mercury tension in our birthchart. Neptune represents imagination, art, music, and other forms of creativity. These artistic avenues have, historically, been the one positive option for homosexuals in our society. This has been the one place where the two sides could somewhat co-exist. Straight society could handle open homosexuality in the form of Liberace for example.

In the 1960's and 70's things began to change. Along with the so-called 'sexual revolution' in the mainstream culture, there was a change in attitude within the gay community. Things which had been hidden and suppressed by the dominant repressive culture suddenly found the freedom and power to be expressed. In the homosexual community it appeared as 'gay pride' and 'gay activism'.

I was living in San Francisco in the early 1970's. At that time there was a transition beginning to occur. Previously, in the late 60's, the gay population and the 'counter-culture' population were very mixed. There were a lot of straight and gay 'mixed' bars. In the early 70's it was clear that a new influx of homosexual population was occurring, accompanied by an increased power and public expression. The homosexual community had started to find its 'voice,' its freedom from repression, and in San Francisco especially, a strength in numbers. They were also absorbing some of the darker elements Plutonian elements, such as an overindulgence in physical passion, which is separate from true love and affection. Pursuit of such passion fueled the emergence of the notorious bath houses where gay men could experience multiple partners in one night. During this period, in my observation, there seemed to be few exclusive, committed gay relationships. As the repressed Plutonian intensity within the homosexual population came to the surface, gay persons began to own their collective power and started to 'flaunt it' in the face of straight America.

I should say here that I am not gay. During my time in San Francisco I became friends with a lot of gay people. Since that time a significant number of my clients have been gay. To be homosexual in this society is not an easy path to deal with psychologically. There are so many tensions one has to deal with in relation to the hostile, repressive views and judgments of the mainstream culture. It is understandable that as this Plutonian power started to rise within the homosexual population that it would tend to go into the other extreme of obsession. The rising Plutonian intensity emboldened gays to confront the fearful, limited views of the mainstream society. They began to make the mainstream society itself into the confused, mentally blurred, Mercury in Cancer element. Just as this power and passion was starting to really accumulate, however, it met with a new Plutonian power with a 'life and death' intensity related to their experience of sexuality. It took the form of AIDS.

The clearest information on AIDS I have seen was presented by a particular entity named Lazaris. He exists on a higher plane of existence and has been communicating to us here through a 'channel' or 'medium'. Lazaris specifies three main groups who have generally been the most likely to be afflicted with AIDS. These three groups are Black Africans, where AIDS is a heterosexual disease and not a homosexual disease, intravenous drug users, and homosexual men. Lazaris makes an astute comment on AIDS. He says that if AIDS was God's way of showing who his chosen people were, then it would be clear that God's chosen people were Lesbians. That is the one group which has very little incidence of AIDS. Lazaris goes on to say that he doesn't think that that is what *those people* are trying to imply. The one issue all three groups have in common is defensive-defenselessness. Black

Africans may feel either defenseless in relation to the former colonial powers or the military regimes who now rule their nations, or they feel an overriding defensiveness in their self-rule, perhaps taking part in those military regimes. Intravenous drug users may feel either defenseless in their ability to cope with mainstream reality, or feel defensive when offered help out of their drug induced escapism. Homosexual men may feel either a sense of defenselessness in relation to the homophobia of mainstream society or an over-weaning defensiveness in relation to that homophobia. Lazarus says that either one of these will affect the individual's natural ability to defend themselves. On the physical level this would affect the immune system.

AIDS is a worldwide phenomenon. It appeared while Pluto was moving through Scorpio, the sign related to sex and death. AIDS has clearly put a Plutonian, life or death dimension upon our experience of sexuality, especially indiscriminate sex, whether gay or heterosexual.

The gay community has tended to experience the Pluto/Mercury tension in the U.S. birthchart as an either/or situation. Either they felt their sexuality was repressed by Pluto and they had to stay in the Mercurial 'closet' and repress their sexuality or at least conceal their public expression of it. Or they could become Pluto, indulge in the bath house passion, and 'flaunt' their sexuality at the Mercurial, repressed, homophobic straight society.

The epidemic of AIDS undermined the Plutonian power and passion in the Gay community. Fortunately there is a positive option available in relation to this Pluto vs. Mercury tension. That positive option is from the positive aspects to both Pluto and Mercury by Neptune. There has been an incredible outflow of the positive qualities of Neptune in the gay community. The level of care and compassion has risen dramatically within that community in response to the horrors of AIDS. The life and death Plutonian reality of AIDS clearly cut through the bath-house passion. It has been replaced by a much greater incidence of emotional commitment and love in gay relationships. Within the general mainstream society I think there has been a much greater emergence of Neptunian care and compassion arising in relation to the homosexual community. Obviously, we still have a long way to go, as evidenced by the fundamentalist Christian homophobes who are trying to usurp the ultimate power and control of Pluto for themselves, in 'biblical dimensions'.

Sex and Violence

There is another area where sex, death, money, and power combine with and also manifest 'fuzzy thinking'. This is the area of sex and violence in film, television, and advertising. The easiest way to get someone's attention, with little effort or creative talent at all, is with images of sex or violence. The number of people killed on television witnessed by the average American child by the age of 12 is staggering. It is also sick. Everyone knows it. This assault is allowed to continue through the greed, competition, power, and 'fuzzy thinking' of everyone concerned, including the American public. I sympathize with the French and other nations who are trying to limit the amount of American television that is broadcast to their society. Our entertainment industry of course, is resisting these efforts under the banner of 'free trade'.

In 1985 there were 75 million hard-core pornographic video rentals in the U.S. In 1992 that number had risen to 490 million. By 1996 it was 665 million. The percentage of all websites on the Internet devoted to pornography is also staggering. The sheer scale of that much business and money guarantees that nothing will be done to change it. It's too big and too powerful, i.e. 'Plutonian'. Although pornography does exist in other nations, the U.S. is the major producer and exporter. The number of Americans who now admit to being literally addicted to pornography, to the extent that they are socially dysfunctional, is also staggering. Talk about 'muddying up the reasoning ability'! It has been reported that in 1999 the Xerox company fired a considerable number of employees for spending up to eight hours a day viewing internet pornographic websites. There we have again sex, power, money, control, all mixed-up together.

I am not sure what we should or could do about this situation. We could demand controls on internet pornography to prohibit e-mail advertising of 'barely legal teen sluts' and 'barnyard bestiality'. Personally, I enjoy sex, but if I don't have a romantic partner in my life, I don't want to be overtly sexually stimulated. And if I have a lover in my life, I don't need pornography. Spiritual teachers have taught that the images from pornography, which get lodged in your psyche, literally plague you psychically with unfulfilled lust. It's not a happy place to be. Just think of serial murderer Ted Bundy, who claimed that the frustrations he felt from watching hard-core pornography are what fueled his acts of violence and murder.

There has been a study made in Denmark, the country which was the first European nation to repeal its anti-obscenity laws. That study indicated that, after an initial increase of interest in pornography, there has now been a slow, steady decline. I would like to think that men in our society can start to grow up us well. However, I don't think that Denmark has this same Pluto/Mercury tension. Our birthchart reflects an immature, sexually uncertain, confused Mercury in the Eighth House, which is in opposition to a secret, hidden, intense and passionate Pluto in the Second House. When these ingredients are blended in with greed and money we are faced with quite a challenge.

Commentary by U.S. News and World Report correspondent Eric Schlosser parallels my observations:

> Critics of the sex industry have long attacked it for being "un-American"—and yet there is something quintessentially American about it: The heady mix of sex and money, the fortunes quickly made and lost, the new identities assumed and then discarded, the public condemnations of a private obsession. Largely fueled by loneliness and frustration, the sex industry has been transformed from a minor subculture on the fringes of society into a major component of American popular culture.[3]

What bothers me more is how we are spreading pornography around the world through the Internet. The internet, neutral in itself, can deliver positive content, such as our passion for free speech. The internet is said to be one of the major supports for the democratic movement in China. This media also deliver a growing tide of negative content. I have a friend from Paris, who lives part of each year in Bali. She would walk past a garage in her village and see 10-20 teenage boys and young men standing for hours, every day, watching pornography on the Internet. This is a scene which is occurring all over the world wherever a computer and a modem can be plugged in. Pornography is now invading cultures which have never been exposed to that kind of energy before.

The profusion of American produced pornography helps me understand why fundamentalist elements in the world feel that their backs are up against the wall as American secular culture encroaches upon them. I am reminded of Jerry Falwell's comment that the 9/11 tragedy was a result of the secularization of American society. Personally, I think it was extremely insensitive for him to have said that, especially at that time in that way. I must admit, however, I am somewhat in sympathy with what he said. I think if it was just freedom and democracy which we were exporting to the world at large, the terrorists wouldn't have quite the same 'charge'. As people in foreign nations watch their societies inundated by the worst aspects of American society: titillating sex, obsessive violence, and an American culture based on greed, well yes, one could sympathize.

Americans and Sex

The evolution of sexuality is a subject of deep significance in all nations and cultures. The Astrological configuration within the U.S. birthchart indicates that our experiences relative to sexuality would be subject to profound tension and transformation. The Astrological configuration is, once again, Pluto in the Second House, the Taurean house of money and resources, but also of love and sexuality, opposite to Mercury. Mercury is in the Eighth House, the Scorpio-related house of sex, birth and death. The fact that Pluto, the planet of complete transformation which you cannot avoid, is opposite to the only other planet related specifically to sexuality in the birthchart, in itself, would indicate a particularly intense karmic energy involved in the area of sexual experience.

We have already examined the intensity of this Pluto/Mercury opposition within the specific topics of abortion, homosexuality, sex and violence, and pornography. Now I would like to address the topic of sexuality within the larger society. In my observation, there is an over-riding psychological dynamic which lies behind the American experience of sexuality. This dynamic is relatable to the Mercury/Pluto opposition under discussion here. The source of this psychological dynamic is the long term results of what I call 'Puritanism'. I define Puritanism as religious insistence on purity which tended to suppress the enjoyment of natural instinctual passions such as sexuality. This is an ailment which afflicted many societies and nations. It was especially prevalent in Northern European nations, but an acute form of it spread through the 'Anglo' nations, such as Britain, Canada, the U.S., Australia and New Zealand. It brings to mind a well-known story of Queen Victoria. When she was asked, by either her daughter or some female relative, how she should approach the experience of sexuality, Queen Victoria instructed her to "Just lie down and think of England dear." I have a friend from England whose mother always told her "Sex is nothing but a duty I've never enjoyed". My friend said this conditioning upon her was so bad that she had to leave England to have sex the first time. She went to Paris.

Hilarion has said that the original intent in encouraging individuals to refrain from sex before marriage was to allow the sexual energy to build up and move upwards, into the higher 'heart chakra' area. He goes on to say that with this encouragement, however, it was never intended to result in a demeaning of, or a rejection of, the pleasure of the sex act itself. I would say that this was a rather major cultural 'backfire'.

If I were to examine each nation's Astrological birthchart, I believe I would see the individual ways in which each would be likely to play out their sexual karma. In the case of the U.S., we have this Mercury in the Eighth house, the Scorpio-related house of sex, birth, and death, opposite to Pluto. Pluto is one of the two planets which 'rule' the sign Scorpio. The dynamics of this opposition, again, appears in many different ways in the American experience. One way in which this Mercury/Pluto opposition surfaces in the American experience of sexuality is where the Mercury in Cancer, 'muddied up thinking,' along with the Mercury in the Eighth House 'feelings of sexual frustration' combine in this Puritanical repression and denial of sexuality. This denial and repression, however, results in compulsive, secret, hidden, illicit, passion. Compulsive, secret, hidden, illicit are all qualities of the potentially darker side of Pluto.

A good example of this tension is Jimmy Swaggart, the Evangelical Preacher who was caught more than once soliciting the services of prostitutes. Here we have Evangelical 'purity,' with the Mercurial characteristics described above, unable to resist his 'demons,' with the Plutonian characteristics described above. This kind of scenario may appear in other nations, but it does have a distinctly American character to it. A more recent manifestation has been the Catholic priest sexual abuse scandals. One could surmise that if such abuse was taking place on the same scale in other countries there would have been a similar outcry.

This Mercurial Puritanical Repression vs. Plutonian Passion appears in all kinds of American phenomenon. For example, the moral outrage in Congress over President Clinton's sexual indulgence contrasted to the panic which went through Washington when *Hustler Magazine* founder Larry Flint offered $1 million to anyone who had evidence of illicit passion among congressmen. This fear of public scandal led to one congressman resigning, admitting he had 'strayed' from his marriage. I am sure we can all cite numerous instances of this Puritan vs. Passion dichotomy in the American experience. Most Europeans, however, in observation of this theme in America tend to think that we are rather 'nuts'.

Familial Sexual Abuse

Another manifestation of this Puritan vs. Passion tension is the alarming incidence of sexual abuse in families. In my counseling practice I ask 30-45 minutes of questions about an individual's life before I start to provide insight into the experiences which have and are happening in their lives in the context of the Astrological factors in their birthchart. After having conducted many of these interviews, country to country, I have come to observe different psychological patterns and statistics within different nations. Sexual abuse appears everywhere, but there is a much higher incidence of it, in my observation, in the U.S. than European nations. European nations have their sexual pathological behaviors, yet they just seem to play out differently, such as rampant infidelity.

There are a variety of factors which can be involved in this abusive behavior. Noted Astrologer and Jungian Analyst Liz Greene once stated that difficult Pluto/Mars aspects show up a high percentage of times in the birthcharts of both rapists and rape victims. For both parties it is an experience of the negative effects of selfishly indulged lust. There does seem to be Astrological corollaries relatable at times to the experience of the karma involved in these incidents.

Why this high incidence of familial sexual abuse in this country? I have my own theory. My theory relates to the understanding that there is a natural attraction between the sexes. This will include mothers and sons, fathers and daughters. In a 'Puritanical' society, which is so hung up about the body and sexuality and where the incest 'taboo' is so strong, this quite natural energy gets repressed. Again, we have Mercury in Cancer 'muddied up thinking' and Mercury in the Eighth House 'sexual frustration' trying to resist Plutonian, instinctual energy. When Pluto is not allowed to manifest in a positive way, such as deep regenerative connection with love, however, it will manifest in a negative way, such as betrayal, autocratic control and manipulation, and/or selfishly-indulged passion, i.e. incest.

Sex Before and After 10 PM

However much our mainstream, socio-cultural presentation may seem sexually 'liberated,' to me it still has a very Mercury in Cancer 'muddied up thinking'. Our national persona is equally impaired by our Mercury in the Eighth House, 'sexually frustrated' character. These two characteristics inhibit our connection to the deeper Plutonian potential of the experience of sexuality. Sure we have lots of sex on TV. But it is either shows of 'psycho' rape and murder sex scenes after 10 PM, or the silliest, childish, sexual innuendos flaunted every other minute on the television sit-coms before 10 PM. The murder and sex scenes are Pluto in its darkest form. The sitcoms embody the Mercurial, 'muddied up thinking,' and silliness. It is a silliness which denies or inhibits the potential for Plutonian, deep regeneration of the Soul. What is missing is the healing influence of Neptune on both ends of this Pluto/Mercury tension. This Neptunian quality, once discovered, could unite sexual passion with true unconditional love and sacred spirituality. The fact that Neptune is there and available to this Pluto/Mercury tension is a hopeful sign. We have the opportunity to move beyond Mercurial, Puritanical repression and Plutonian obsession by healing and integrating the sexual experience with deep, vulnerable, Neptunian compassionate surrender.

America and its Sexual Roles

The personal and social roles experienced by men and women is another topic which is universal in scope. There is an overall global, archetypal, and evolutionary transformation taking place on this planet in relation to the sexual roles. It is likely that the experience of the sexual roles in this country would involve a particular transformative intensity specifically relatable to the symbolic energies involved in our Mercury/Pluto opposition. All nations have their own path of transformation, but if we were to compare men and women of the 1940's and 50's in this country with the men and women of today, there seems to be a more extreme degree of transformation than, say, in the European nations.

In this regard, there is a statement heard in this country which I rarely hear in other nations. That statement being, "I don't know what the sexual roles are anymore or where we are going from here?". Using the U.S. Astrological blueprint and my own psychological/sociological observations, I will share my personal assessments of this aspect of American experience. This is a topic which engenders a high degree of commentary in this nation. On the obsessive ends of the spectrum we have, on the one hand, some of the most extreme forms of feminism, where I actually read that the psychological/spiritual health of the nation would be improved if women stopped having boy babies for ten years. And on the other end of this spectrum, we have the most entrenched patriarchal outrages such as talk radio host Rush Limbaugh's diatribes against the 'feminazis'. Without venturing into a lengthy exploration of the larger, archetypal picture relative to the global experience of the Masculine and Feminine, which would be the topic for another book, let us look at what has been and is occurring in the United States.

American Women

There is a certain psychological pattern which I have observed in 'readings' I have performed for clients over the years. In this particular reading I do using Tarot cards, there are two positions which are highly significant. One represents the individual's inner, archetypal experience of, and relationship to, the masculine principle. The other is the individual's inner archetypal experience of, and relationship to the feminine principle. The pattern I have observed is that, in most of the readings which I do for women, especially in this country, the masculine card in the reading is stronger and is more identified with than the feminine side. In America this is the case in approximately 18 out of 20 readings. This masculine identification of American women was apparent when I lived in Europe. In Europe I could often tell an American woman walking down the street, before she said a word, just by how she walked…with a semi-aggressive, square-edged, assertive masculine energy, which was noticeably different from the walk of a European woman.

112

I believe this masculine identification happens for at least one of three main reasons. If the first two reasons don't relate to the individual woman, the third one virtually always does. The first reason occurs when a woman, as a child, is not in a close relationship with her mother. The relationship with the mother is a major way in which a girl normally learns what a woman is, through the role model of the mother. And if she rejects that role model, it makes it more difficult for her to know what a woman is, in which case she may develop the masculine as a source of identity.

The second reason occurs when a woman, as a child, is not in a close or trusting relationship with her father. That is another major way for a girl to experience her femininity, through the polarity of reflection from a man. Normally the father is the first man whom she trusts enough to experience the vulnerability of being female. If she doesn't feel that trust she may again develop the masculine, not only as a source of identity, but also as a source of protection from the father.

And the third reason, the one which tends to always affect women, even if the first two didn't, is that modern life seems to be desperately trying to turn everyone into men. It is the traditional masculine qualities of work, career and intellectual pursuit which are highly valued. In contrast, the traditional feminine qualities of emotional relatedness and mothering are of secondary or inferior value today. This disparity tends to be quite prevalent in the 'Anglo' countries of Britain, Canada, and the U.S. This devaluation of women's roles is traceable to the long term results of 'Puritanism,' which represented a time when it was difficult for a woman to physically enjoy being a woman. Puritans dressed in severe clothing and repressed the display of emotions; for a woman to admit that she enjoyed sexuality was to be considered 'cheap,' immoral, and low. A woman's traditional role was diminished while the longstanding barriers to pursue masculine goals of work, career, and intellect remained intact. She was expected to have babies, but to not enjoy making them, and to exhibit no intelligence.

Women's awareness of the restrictive Puritan tradition has grown in the past 50 years, resulting in increased resentment and efforts to pursue traditional careers. Everyone should have the freedom to explore the male and female aspects of themselves, which we all have in varying degrees. However, there has been such a collective compulsivity in this masculinization of women that it hasn't allowed women to see what they are really missing. It has been hard to see because it has been missing for hundreds, if not thousands of years. Women and men have suffered from losing the awareness and appreciation of the powerful and sacred feminine. The degree of masculinization among women does change from country to country. For example, in France, even though the Church tried to tell them that sex was bad, clearly few people in France actually believed it. All of the Christian Churches in the world, Protestant and Catholic, had a repressive attitude towards sexuality. This has resulted in many imbalanced attitudes and behaviors of different kinds in all of the Christianized nations. This Puritan denial of the actual pleasure of the instinctual passion of sexuality never took hold in the Southern European countries of Italy, Spain, Greece, and France, however. It seems that in locales where the physical body is not covered up with lots of clothes due to cold weather for a significant portion of the year, the people seem incapable of actually believing that the pleasure of sex is a bad thing. They may have lots of Catholic guilt about 'illicit sex,' i.e. before marriage, adultery, etc., but not the same denial of the pleasure of the act itself.

Women's Power

In pointing out the masculinization of American women I am not trying to imply that women shouldn't be strong and powerful. I have been inspired by many powerful women teachers. There is a difference, however. If a woman has a very strong card in the feminine side in the Tarot reading, which I mentioned earlier, then that is indicative of a woman with strong power and wisdom as a woman. When she has a weak or dysfunctional card in the feminine, however, and a strong powerful card in the masculine, she may be rather 'possessed,' or taken over by her masculine, unconscious identity. This identification with the masculine may be an effort to escape the fear and woundedness in the feminine, in the, basically, wounded, frightened little girl within. With this psychological pattern within her, she may carry the hope that she will find a man who will live that strong masculine energy for her and in effect 'save' her. However, as long as those wounds, or doubts of worthiness to receive love, exist in the inner child, then the woman will either find someone who validates those doubts, or she will unconsciously project those doubts upon the male partner. The partner will unconsciously react to those doubts, and she will unconsciously sabotage the relationship. It is not uncommon for these two avenues of experiencing the strong masculine with a wounded or weak feminine to occur simultaneously. It is amazing how many women are able to be strong and effective in their work or career, and yet find themselves dominated or even abused in their relationships. The key is in healing the inner wounds.

In the larger collective view of things it seems that before the 1960's Men were Pluto and Women were Mercury. Men had all of the power of Pluto in the Second House, the Taurean house of money and finances, providing them with economic power and control. Men also had the dominant role in sexuality and acted as the 'aggressor'. Women were more Mercurial, in the sense of the Mercury in Cancer, having less mental clarity and sharpness, which is equitable to the much more limited opportunities for education and intellectual development for women at that time. Women were Mercurial also in the sense of Mercury in the Eighth House, that is sexually uncertain and frustrated. This condition is due, again, to the repressive Puritanical relation to sexuality, especially for women.

Obviously, men today still wield more power and control economically, and in many relationships, sexually. However, their power has declined dramatically since the 1960's. In the 60's and 70's women collectively started to own their own Pluto. They started to develop a collective, transformative power and intensity. They started to own and develop their intellect, assertiveness, and physicality, and to not simply let men live these things for them. Through this Plutonian liberation and transformation, American Women have been a great leader and proponent for freedom and equality of opportunity for women throughout the world.

In order to be free of a very repressed feminine role, however, it does seem that it was necessary for the past thirty years for women to go to an extreme masculine polarity. The path now is to find a balance. To regain a quality of feminine power, identity, and wisdom which has been lacking for hundreds if not thousands of years.

An example of a former interactive balance and respect of the differences between male and female power was illustrated in a lecture given by the eminent philosopher and writer Manly P. Hall. He was talking about the previously mentioned Native American Iroquois Six Nations Federation. Mr. Hall said that before the white man came the Iroquois had 600 years of peace. That fact alone is one virtually unheard of in recorded history. At a certain stage in the history of their federation the Iroquois developed a collective governing body of chieftains and sachems from the different tribes and bands. All of these positions could only be held by men. No women were allowed to hold one of these positions of governing power. However, the men were all elected in elections in which only women could vote. The women still had their own circle, but its' purpose was not to travel here and there for political discussion, or to determine where the boundaries of the hunting grounds should be demarcated. When the women came together it was more for spiritual ceremony. Any man who stepped out of line in the observance of his duty, however, could be taken out of office in 24 hours by a unanimous vote of the women. The Iroquois balanced the men's daily rule with the women's ultimate determining power.

This was clearly a time when men and women had clearly defined roles. Such distinct roles are no longer appropriate for our times. The point I am making here is that we have lost, worldwide, this respect for women's unique wisdom. It is the respect which would allow Iroquois men to submit to the decision making power of women, and a self-respect within women which did not feel belittled or competitive with men. Women taking on men's power, economically and politically, may allow changes to occur, but not if they succumb to the same abuses of control and power which men are heir to.

In this regard I would like to share the following comments of Marianne Williamson:

> As women, we need to do more than just enter the halls of financial or governmental power. We must do something much more difficult than that: we must change things once we get there. How co-opted we have been in the last thirty years, breaking through glass ceilings, only to go to lunch and then out shopping. Feminism is a failure if ultimately all it means is that women have the same right to worldly power as men have. The higher significance of power is not the struggle to attain it but, rather, what we do with it. The feminist perspective in society should stand to remind us that the *point* of power is to make the world a better place. And that means something much, much more than just making some people richer.[4]

As in all of the previous discussions of the Pluto/Mercury oppositional tensions within the U.S. birthchart, relative to money, abortion, homosexuality, etc., the Astrological factor available to heal and integrate the either/or components of this tension is the 'sextile' and 'trine' positive aspects from the planet Neptune. Neptune is making positive aspects to both the Mercury and the Pluto. Women's dichotomy between Mercurial, relative powerlessness, and Plutonian control and domination can only be healed and integrated through a Neptunian compassion, forgiveness, and spiritually surrendered healing. A compassion for the frightened, wounded little girls within. A compassion for the frightened little boys within men, knowing that the most macho, patriarchal, aggressive man is the most insecure, frightened little boy within. There must be trust and faith that there is a higher purpose and plan unfolding through all of the pain, confusion, and misery.

For those of us who believe in reincarnation, we cannot look at what is happening in the world today as simply what present day men are doing to present day women. We have all been each other's victim and victimizer. However, why does this universally occurring subjugation of women by men appear in virtually all cultures? One reason is because of the lack of true surrendered spirituality. For men to deny any need to surrender and to be humbly vulnerable to the spiritual source from which life comes, and to maintain the illusion of security in their own intellect and material power creates a situation whereby men also must deny any need to surrender and to be vulnerable to the physical source from which life comes. This denial leads to a subjugation of women, those who give us life. It also leads to a subjugation of the Earth herself, another Mother which gives birth to all that we are and have.

The intensity of the Pluto/Mercury opposition makes the U.S. a leader in transforming the old sexual roles. The question is where do we go with this transformative capacity.

American Men

So far this discussion has primarily considered the female experience in America. This is largely because the transformation of women in American society has been more dramatic. To compare the men of the 1950's with men of today reveals a less radical transformation than that of women of the 50's compared to the women of today. American men have gone through many transformations of their own, however, and they have the distinct experience of learning how to adapt to the radical changes which have occurred within women.

Compared with European men, I would say that American men have previously developed a more distinctly masculine identity. We are a nation of rugged frontiersmen with our John Wayne and 'Rambo' stereotypes. Whereas European men are from much more urban, cosmopolitan or stable agricultural communities. The polarity between men and women in the U.S. in the fifties was not as strong in Europe. I think women in Europe retained more self-respect and individual, if not socio-economic and political, power. European men exhibited more of a balance of masculine with feminine qualities. Personally, I am rather physically thin. Among European men I never feel in any way 'effeminate' compared to how I may feel among many American men. This difference between European masculinity and American masculinity is evident today in the American military which tends to feel itself much more capable than the militaries in other European nations, refusing to place American troops under foreign commanders.

This strong dominant masculine identity among American men has been one cause of the rebellion and transformation of American women. The question is: What is happening now with American men?

I have fewer male clients than female clients. This is a common statistic among all therapeutic modalities. Basically, males are trained to be independent and self-reliant. Females are more geared towards a dependence on others for their well-being. Additionally, there also tends to be many more women drawn to the more spiritual or mystical dimensions of things such as Astrology, etc.

Most of the men whom I do see as clients, however, come from a similar background in that as children they were closer emotionally to their mothers than to their fathers. One could say that perhaps men with the opposite background, having been closer to their fathers than to their mothers, would be the kind of men who would be less likely to seek outside therapeutic help. This lack of deep emotional connection between sons and fathers is a collective phenomenon. It began with the industrial revolution, where fathers went away to work and mothers raised the children. In this country this disconnection seems to be more prevalent and extreme than in the other industrialized nations.

One reason that fathers would be less available to their sons is observable in the birthchart tension between Pluto and Mercury. Mercury is a planet which, according to Hilarion, is also relatable to the child phase of development. We have already identified men, in general, with Plutonian power and control. Pluto in the Second House, the Taurean house of money and finances, has been portrayed as a cause for the economic and material obsession in America. It is partly the material obsession of American males which has cut fathers off from being available emotionally for their children. It has allowed fathers to think that just being a 'breadwinner,' providing financial support, was all that was required of them. This is a pattern which exists among men of all industrialized nations, but it is much more extreme here. For example, people in Europe are dumfounded that we Americans allow ourselves, on average, only two weeks of vacation time per year. In Europe the average is four to six weeks of vacation time. This obsessive, materialistic work ethic doesn't allow time for working fathers to deeply bond with their children.

This abandonment of sons by their fathers has been pointed out by many observers, including feminist writer Susan Faludi in her book: *Stiffed: The Betrayal of the American Man*, which is based on many conversations with American men. The work of Robert Bly and other proponents of the 'Men's Movement,' also acknowledge this lack of positive male mentoring between fathers and sons in our society.

This lack of generational connection between sons and fathers, however, can also be seen as a necessary stage in an over-all positive process of transformation. The most acute separation between fathers and sons in this country took place in the 1960's during the Vietnam anti-war and cultural revolutionary movements of that time. Our fathers marched with World War II mentality, when might was right, into the much more complex and confusing 'quagmire' of Vietnam. They were carrying on with the previously predominant male paradigm of America. Their children, however, whose fathers were off to work with only two weeks vacation, were more than ever raised by their mothers. This disconnect from fathers, resistance to the war, and counter-culture explosion allowed these children to own their own Pluto. It allowed them to refute the unquestioning economic, political, and militaristic values of the traditional American male paradigm. This generational divide and 1960's cultural revolution occurred in many nations, but here it was more extreme. This Pluto/Mercury opposition is one factor which would explain the extremity of the experience here. The elder American male is observable as the obsessive, dominant Pluto, willing to send boys not old enough to vote off to die. These boys are observable as the Mercurial and mentally confused children of these fathers. Mercury is in the Eighth House, the Scorpio-related house of sex, birth and death. However, many of these boys turned the energies around and themselves became Pluto. With their new Plutonian intensity they burned their draft cards, marched in huge masses against the 'Establishment,' and towards the end of the War in Vietnam they posed a great threat to their own officers. This role reversal had some of the darker Plutonian elements, where bombings and even murder seemed justified. With this Pluto/Mercury opposition in our birthchart, we do tend to go from one extreme to the other.

American Men Today

Where does this leave men today, psychologically, with this disconnect from our fathers? Personally, I think it was necessary for us to experience this male to male disconnection in order to allow a new paradigm the possibility of unfolding. We also have to be aware of what we have lost in the process. As I stated earlier, most men I see as clients were closer emotionally to their mothers than to their fathers. Of the men who do come to see me, they tend to fall in one of two groups. Both of these groups, through their closeness with their mothers, have the potential for a connection to a feminine, emotional capacity for sensitivity and relatedness. The first category of men were those who were able to consciously accept and even identify with this feminine energy. This may occur in such a way that there is a dissociation from their male energy and identity, however.

The second category of men are those who also had this strong connection with the mother, but because of the socio-cultural environment in which they grew up or other dynamics within the home, never felt safe enough to consciously accept and identify with this feminine energy. In such cases this feminine consciousness and energy is pushed into the unconscious, and their way of accessing it is by finding a woman who will live it for them, upon whom they can 'project' it. As with women, there can be a hope within a man to be 'saved' by a woman. But again, if this hope is to compensate for wounds or doubts of worthiness to receive love in the inner child and inner masculine self, he will either find a woman who validates those doubts, or he will unconsciously project them upon her.

These two groups of my clients tend to split along generational lines. Older men, those born before 1947 or so, tend to be in the second category. Before the 1960's, when men born after 1947 would have been roughly in their teens, it wasn't very easy for a man to identify with and exhibit feminine qualities. Younger men, however, tend to be in the first category, which results in a tendency towards a similar kind of unconscious 'possession' as with women. In the case with men this would be the inner feminine identity. To be noted here is that just because a man is open to his feminine side doesn't necessarily make it 'nice'. The anima, the inner feminine archetypal identity within a man, when based on fear or rejection of the masculine inner child, or little boy self, can be rather 'bitchy'.

For the soft, sensitive men who have relinquished the negative aspects of Plutonian dominance, power, and control, but in doing so may have sacrificed their Plutonian 'intensity, passion, and joy' of being a man I recommend reading 'Iron John' by author Robert Bly. Iron John is an ancient fairytale which Bly uses to illustrate the need for the young male to connect with the deep masculine. This is a masculine which doesn't have to be 'macho,' but can nonetheless be rooted in a life-giving primal 'yang' male energy. Such energy can have a positive, respectful relationship with the feminine, both within himself and within his relationships with women.

There is within America an on-going tension between the two archetypal male roles under discussion here. The rather aggressive, disconnected from the feminine, maleness, contrasted to a somewhat effeminate, lacking in a more profound rooted connection to the masculine, maleness. The swing between these two American masculine models is evident in our presidential choices. After Nixon and Ford, rather masculine, we elected Carter, more feminine, then back to Reagan and George Bush Sr., more masculine, then to Clinton, more feminine, then to George Bush Jr., more masculine. Again, the answer to this oppositional energy is the healing integration of the two extremes. And, once again, the healing, compassionate spiritually surrendered component of Neptune is what is available in our birthchart to embrace, heal and integrate these and all the other Pluto/Mercury tensions. A healing which could allow men and women to face each other without fear, straight and gay without fear, elders and youth without fear. Such compassion would reveal a nation based on love in its purest form.

Beyond Romantic Love

To really heal all of the repression/obsession, power/control, male and female issues we will have to open to a depth of Neptunian experience beyond what was previously known in this nation or perhaps the world. During the 1960's cultural revolution, the planet Pluto, that 'great bringer of change' was conjuncting by 'transit' our natal Neptune. This Pluto transit deepened and empowered Neptune's potential to provide balance, healing, and integration of our Mercury/Pluto tensions of all kinds. There was a transformation of psychological identities among women, young people, and homosexuals. A transformation of much of the general collective society was initiated at that time. We are obviously far from finished, however.

One way to really heal the repressive, obsessive, 'muddied up thinking,' power, and control issues would be to go beyond our infatuation with romantic love. There is an excellent book by the American psychologist Robert Johnson titled *We: The Psychology of Romantic Love*. In his own way, using the myth of Tristan and Isolde, Johnson convincingly argues that one of the major psychological ailments of western culture is romantic love. It is what every novel, every movie, and every pop song is about. This situation exists because we have such a dearth of opportunity for any kind of true experience of spiritual transcendence, wholeness, and unity. Other nations who still maintain mystical practices and traditions provide other opportunities for this kind of transcendent wholeness. I have personally spoken with author Robert Johnson and he told me he had been accepted as a member of a village in India where he spends six months of the year. He said he has to go there to get away from what he calls the 'wounded feeling function' of the West. He says that the Western Society's capacity for true emotional experience is severely wounded because we are so predominately mental, rational, and logical in our relationship to life. Whereas in India he finds that their emotional and spiritual life is quite healthy. He did point out that their <u>thinking</u> isn't so well developed. To have a government that works and to figure out how to get enough to eat is their challenge. He also stated that this wholesome emotional/spiritual capacity is the case with traditional Indians, not so much among those Indians who are largely westernized.

For us westerners, with our powerful mental and rational bias, the only place where we can experience even a taste of transcendent wholeness is romantic love. However, this destroys our capacity for true human relationship. This is because no human can carry that load of transcendent wholeness for you. Beyond the honeymoon, a mere human cannot serve as the true complementary, healing wholeness of your deepest being and psyche. The story of the fairytale Prince and Princess living happily ever after is really symbolic of uniting the male and female within oneself. A uniting of conscious and unconscious, a uniting of individuality with the allness of the Divine.

Neptune is the planet related to that true spiritual, mystical oneness, which could heal our obsessions around sex, money, power, control, and security. The fact that the U.S. has Neptune in positive aspect to both ends of this Pluto/Mercury oppositional tension indicates that the potential to bring deep healing and compassion is there. This potential explains why a large segment of Americans have long been seeking the opportunities for spiritual experience in foreign traditions, as well as within the mystical roots of our own western traditions.

There was Neptunian spirituality in the spiritual vision of the founders of our nation. Native Americans had it, and many still have it. Many of us are now seeking it. There are, however, reasons why true Neptunian spirituality, compassion, and healing are still hard for us Americans to fully embrace in a clear and coherent way. These reasons will be examined in the next chapter.

1   *More Answers,* Hilarion, pp. 89-90.

2   *Astrology Plus,* Hilarion, pp. 120-121.

3   *The Business of Porn,* Eric Schlosser, U.S. News & World Report, February 10, 1997.

4   *The Healing of America,* Marianne Williamson, p. 226.

6

6

SPIT-BALLS AND RELATIONSHIPS

I have spoken previously about Mars in Gemini in the U.S. birthchart and the impact of its powerful mental energy. I have also spoken about Neptune as a potential source for empathy, compassion, and spirituality. However, I have not yet spoken about the fact that Mars and Neptune are 'square', in tension with each other, in our birthchart. This tension is the last of the three major sources of conflict and tension within the U.S. birthchart we will examine. The two previous tense aspects we reviewed are the Saturn/Jupiter square and the Pluto/Mercury opposition.

The purpose of investigating the tense/difficult aspects between planets in a birthchart is to reveal and explain their influences. This information, however disturbing or negative it may appear, in fact provides the necessary awareness for the individual or nation to integrate and heal these sources of tension within itself. Once these tensions are dealt with then the individual or nation has far greater access to the positive energies available in their birthchart. Furthermore, it is the conflicts within us which create the dynamism and drama in our lives that force us to grow and evolve. As I said earlier, the only way to heal and integrate these tensions is to attune to a transpersonal, soul level of consciousness. It is only from that 'Higher Self' perspective that one can embrace the seeming dichotomies within oneself.

The Mars/Neptune square, as with the other tensions within our chart, has expressed itself in a variety of layers and levels within the American experience. This tension also shares similarities with the scenarios of difficulty and conflict previously examined. The Mars/Neptune tension, however, does add its own dimension to the discussion.

In our birthchart, the Mars end of this tension is in the Astrological sign Gemini. Mars in Gemini, difficultly aspected, as by this square to Neptune, will manifest in the following traits:

> There is....a tendency for the afflicted Mars in Gemini to be mentally or verbally combative or abusive. The strife and pugnaciousness of the afflicted Mars will, if in Gemini, tend to make the person seek out situations in which verbal spats and abusiveness will manifest. [1]

This mental, verbal contentiousness is definitely a significant characteristic of our society. In his book *The Sibling Society*, author Robert Bly argues that we Americans have lost a capacity for true respect for any kind of higher authority, or even a willingness to embody a quality of authority or wisdom. By maligning or shirking authority as adults, we have in effect become a society of 'siblings'. As I see it, we are a society of clever, critical, self-styled 'pundits', who are infatuated with our own cutting edge intellectual disdain and commentary. It is clear that the belligerent nature of these traits is directly attributable to this difficultly aspected Mars in Gemini, and its "tendency....to be mentally or verbally combative or abusive".

What really aggravates, even threatens, the critical, intellectual Gemini Mars presence in our chart is the tension with spiritual, mystical Neptune. Located in the Ninth House, which is concerned with philosophy and religion, Neptune's birthchart placement is squarely in tension with Mars in Gemini. This explains why anything spiritual or mystical is very likely to be criticized in this society. The intensity of this square is illustrated by Mars in Gemini's automatic, knee-jerk reaction to anything Neptunian, positive or negative. The positive qualities of Neptune are empathy, compassion, deep trust and faith. The negative qualities of Neptune include confusion, illusion, delusion, victimhood, and martyrdom. The powerful influence of the negative aspects of Neptunian mysticism upon our society is illustrated by our propensity to embrace wacky spiritual movements and disturbing cults which the more sophisticated Europeans would never believe in. These kinds of delusionary spirituality are threatening and antagonistic to the Mars in Gemini intellectual identity.

The problem with squares and oppositions, such as this Neptune square to Mars in Gemini, is their tendency to create either/or situations. In this case, either you can be religious and spiritual, i.e. Neptune, but lacking any clear, effective intellectual capability. Or you can be intelligent and clever, i.e. Mars in Gemini, but lacking compassion and faith in a power greater than your own intellect. A good example of this tension is the clash between New Age spirituality and the mainstream media. Admittedly, portions of New Age thought and practice, especially in this country, exhibit Neptunian illusion and 'flakiness'. Because of the either/or polarization, however, the mainstream media is compelled to cynically mock everything branded New Age.

Obviously, our society needs to heal and integrate this tension. We need to be able to discern and select a spirituality which doesn't insult our intelligence. And we need intellectual engagement which drops the 'smart-ass' routine and allows us to open to a deeper trust, faith, and quality of compassion. In the aftermath of 9/11, I was wondering what the witty comics of late night television would be saying. A chastened Jon Stewart of the *Daily Show* was quoted as saying, "I feel like I'm one of the kids in the back of the room throwing spit-balls at everyone up front". Such humility and candor provide hope that we Americans can recognize the negative patterns in our birthchart and act with awareness.

The Victim/Victimizer Program

Another prevalent theme wherever there is Neptune tension in a birthchart is what I call the victim/victimizer program. Essentially, this is a situation where, if you feel you may be victimized but don't want to be a victim, then you have to be a victimizer. If you don't want to be a victimizer, then you have to be a victim. You are only able to see those two choices. There appears to be no way out, at least at that level. The only way out of this behavioral straitjacket is by acknowledging the positive side of Neptune. This means giving yourself the opportunity to experience unconditional love for yourself and for others, and total forgiveness for yourself and for others. Neptune can comfort us with spiritual faith, trust, and the realization that there are no victims or victimizers, but only us frightened little boys and girls trying to do the best that we can.

This victim/victimizer theme is carried within many of America's extremist groups. The Ku Klux Klan and Aryan Nations see themselves as victims of Civil Rights advocates or of a worldwide 'Jewish Conspiracy', so therefore they feel justified in victimizing others. The government assault on religious cult leader David Koresh's compound in Waco, Texas is a good example of confusion over who was the victim and who was the victimizer. Perhaps David Koresh was experiencing his own Neptunian delusions and sought victimhood while victimizing the surrounding federal forces. Meanwhile our government's only response was Martian, feeling it had no choice but to be the victimizer. Neither side was able to pierce the illusion and access Neptunian compassion. Again, a tendency to be either/or, at the extreme ends of the spectrum.

A classic example of our potential for illusionary, mass-hysteria in relation to a perceived enemy whom we feel is victimizing us was the Joseph McCarthy led Anti-Communist crusade in the early 1950's. McCarthy epitomized the negative Mars in Gemini: 'verbally combative or abusive'. Feeling that he and other loyal Americans were being victimized by a vast Communist conspiracy, McCarthy then felt justified in destroying people's careers. He pressured these people to collaborate, forcing them to, in turn, victimize their colleagues. McCarthy did this by forcing them to give up names of 'Communists' to his investigating committee. If people refused they were jailed, often without trial.

Interestingly, Neptune's qualities of creativity and illusion have led it to being attributed with the discovery of photography and the rise of the film industry. Much of Joseph McCarthy's paranoia was directed toward a fear that there were Communists in Hollywood, who were putting Communist propaganda into the psyche of the American public through films. With little proof to warrant his accusations,

McCarthy relied on his abrasive and abusive tactics to fuel the fires of national hysteria. The illusion of Hollywood was trampled by the delusion of McCarthy. Hundreds of film actors, directors, and technicians were blacklisted, with several committing suicide. America was unable to escape the pull of Neptune's victim/victimizer program. Americans began informing on each other all across the nation.

Fortunately McCarthy's delusion blinded his own judgment. He became even more combative and in 1953 brazenly charged that there were Communists in the U.S. Army, including even high ranking officers. He did this even though he had lied about his World War II service record. In addition, McCarthy was an alcoholic (which also relates to Neptune) and that contributed to his delusion and paranoia. President Eisenhower, former commander of the U.S. Military, had had enough and the Army swiftly rebuffed all of McCarthy's claims. In the televised Senate hearings that followed, McCarthy was quickly exposed as the fraudulent bully he was. One could say that through the medium of television Neptune had shown its positive qualities, but the stain of McCarthyism revealed once again the recurring victim/victimizer program in U.S. history.

In the early 1970's Saturn, in the sky, was 'conjuncting' this Mars, and 'squaring' the Neptune. This was the time of 'Watergate'. President Nixon felt he was being victimized by whoever leaked the secret *Pentagon Papers* study to the New York Times, which revealed that our government had consistently lied to the American people about the origins and conduct of the War in Vietnam. Nixon suspected it was Daniel Ellsberg and so he victimized him by wiretapping his telephone and abusing his right to privacy. Nixon also suspected the Democratic Party, so he victimized them by ordering a burglary of their national offices in the Watergate building. This Neptunian, confused invasion of privacy resulted in the media 'victimizing' the President (as Nixon saw it), which justified his lying to the Press, which resulted in Nixon victimizing the public. Eventually it was exposed that Nixon had lied, so he became a bigger victim. This has fairly well set the tone for presidential/media relationship since that time, with the on-going question: who is the real victim and who is the real victimizer?

Interestingly, Nixon himself was born with his Capricorn Sun in opposition to his Neptune in his natal birthchart. This arrangement would give Nixon the desire to be a leader (Capricorn), coupled with a kind of 'savior on a mission' (Neptune) quality. The tension resulting from the opposition between the Sun and Neptune, however, would bring in negative Neptunian qualities, such as confusion, delusion, victimhood, and martyrdom. To add more drama to this potent brew, Nixon's Pluto was in his Tenth House. For this placement Hilarion says:

> Pluto in the tenth denotes one who tends to select a career in which deep-seated problems in his subconscious are to be brought to the surface and dealt with.[2]

Richard Milhouse Nixon's chosen career in politics certainly provided the stage for his 'deep-seated problems' to come to the surface. Additional Astrological forces at play in the Nixon drama were provided by Nixon's Pluto being conjunct to the Mars in the U.S. birthchart. In the powerful Plutonian, Tenth House 'role in the world' that he played as President of the United States of America, Nixon constantly tried to dominate and control the communications of the national media (Mars in Gemini). The media belonged to a host of enemies (real and imagined) that Nixon obsessed about. The victim/victimizer theme was so strong in Nixon because his Plutonian 'role' was also square to the Neptune in the U.S. birthchart. Of course, at the same time that Saturn was conjuncting and squaring the U.S. Mars/Neptune, Saturn was conjuncting Nixon's Pluto. This strong connection between Nixon's Pluto and the Mars/Neptune square would link him personally to the 'victim/victimizer' program in the U.S. birthchart. This was why Nixon was the one fated to personally play out this drama in the American experience. It is a good example of how individual karma can be interlinked with collective karma.

This Neptune/Mars tension affects us in so many unconscious and subliminal ways. It is a major reason why violence is glorified and is so prevalent in American film and television entertainment. As discussed earlier, films are related to Neptune. The Neptune in our birthchart is square to Mars, the god of war. Filmmakers continue to pour money into ever more realistic depictions of gratuitous violence. There isn't any other nation on the earth which watches on their daily television news so many stories of teens and twelve year olds blowing away their classmates in school. American children are twelve times more likely to die of gun violence than in any other Western nation. Something is going on here, and it is full of Martial aggression as well as Neptunian confusion and delusion.

The U.S. And Conflict In Relationships

The Neptunian/Martian, victim/victimizer, illusion, confusion, delusion, and martyrdom also strongly influences how America experiences relationships with other nations. The Mars end of this Mars/Neptune tension is in the Seventh House, the Libra-related house of partnership and relationship. The U.S. birthchart has four planets in this house. It is a large theme in our Astrological karma. Planets situated at the beginning of a house are always stronger in their influence relative to other planets in the house. The U.S. has Mars at the beginning of the Seventh House. Here is what Hilarion says about Mars in the Seventh House:

> The placement of Mars in the seventh house of a birth chart brings the disruptive energies of this planet into the life department dealing with partnerships — particularly the pair-bond partnership with a mate. Mars in the seventh sector tends to promote the selection of a mate who will allow the aggressive and disruptive tendencies of the native to be brought to the surface, where he can clearly see them for what they are, and can experience their results in terms of conflict with the mate. Generally speaking, most of his love-relationships will be marked by conflict energies.

> The lesson is of course to dismantle the tendency to rush into battle when opposed, and to rise above differences on the

wings of true affection. Remember that true love forgives all, and that one of the primary purposes for earth life is to learn at last that true form of compassionate affection. Karmically, the native must pass through repeated episodes in which his love-relationships founder on the shoals of conflict that he himself has created. The pain of separation is a way to discharge burdens accumulated in earlier lives when others suffered similar distress at his hands.[3]

Basically, this placement indicates that the U.S. has a tendency to be aggressive and contentious in how it relates to other nations. As discussed earlier, our ability to see any fault in ourselves as the cause for that aggression is going to be difficult. Such myopia is largely due to Neptunian illusion, confusion, and delusion, as well as some Sagittarian 'seeing ourselves as honest, upright, and morally strong, *whether true or not'*. The U..S. experiences a lot of victim/victimizer in its international relationships. Even when we think we are being the Neptunian healer savior, as we claimed in the Vietnam War, in fact we are experiencing illusion and delusion. The famous comment made by a U.S. commander in Vietnam, "We had to destroy the village in order to save it," brutally illustrates the importance of tempering our Martian aggression with caution and a clear understanding of the facts and some authentic compassion and sensitivity.

Since 1900 the U.S. has become increasingly combative and aggressive in our relationships with other nations, reflecting our Seventh House Mars birthchart placement. In the late 1960's these traits experienced some very intense Plutonian confrontation. The planet Pluto, in the sky, was 'conjuncting' our natal Neptune, which deepened our capacity to embrace sensitivity and compassion. This resulted in the massive anti-war demonstrations, widespread peace movement, and the 'hippie flower child' counterculture.

At the same time, Pluto was squaring our natal Mars. This resulted in the Martial, military quagmire of Vietnam. We went into Vietnam as the aggressive Mars, dropping 7 million tons of bombs (twice what were dropped in all of World War II) on a country the size of

Massachusetts. In reality we were the negative side of Neptune, full of confusion, delusion, and illusion around what we were really doing and why. The Plutonian confrontation manifested in the only war the U.S. ever lost. It provided a 'wake-up' call to indicate that there might be a better way of doing things.

One military person who seemed to have responded to this 'wake-up' call is Retired Rear Admiral Eugene Carroll. Admiral Carroll is a former Assistant Deputy Chief of Naval Operations with 37 years of active duty. His observations of what evolved from that term of military service are quoted here:

> It grew increasingly apparent that wars rarely resolve anything. They may take care of an immediate threat. We dealt with Hitler for example. We semi-solved the situation in Korea. We made a mess out of Vietnam. And I gradually evolved in my thinking to where there has to be an alternative to the war system. We have to find a way for this interdependent world to live together and not resort to violence every 20 or 30 years or so, trying to shoot our way out of problems that have no military solution.

> Believe me I've looked through a lot of bomb sights and I've dropped a lot of bombs and I did a lot of damage. It didn't solve anything. The solutions are far beyond the military's capabilities.[4]

These comments illustrate a positive healing integration between the militaristic capacity of Mars and a Neptunian sensitivity for the actual conditions existing within international relations.

The 1990 Gulf War seemed to indicate that the U.S. did not learn the lesson of the Vietnam War provided by the late 60's Plutonian confrontation. Instead, America viewed the Gulf War as a chance to regain our military pride and to justify our aggressive, contentious manner in dealing with other nations. Personally, it was hard for me to know what was the best course of action in the Gulf War. Being a Libra, I do try to look at things from both sides. I definitely disapprove of Saddam Hussein's aggressivity and repressive regime. However, once the conflict started, the media presentation of it was like the Super Bowl. It seemed to glorify the killing of 100,000 people. I remember a fighter pilot referring to their killing 10,000 Iraqi's that day as being like 'picking pigeons off a fence'.

We absolutely need to get a grip on this Martial combative way of relating to the world. I realize we can't do this by retreating into a Neptunian, delusionary world denying reality. I prefer non-violence, but I cannot deny that Hitler needed to be stopped, or that the Afghan people are better off since the defeat of the Taliban. We need to temper our Martial aggressive manner with the Neptunian sensitivity and compassion that bloomed in the late 1960's. Otherwise we will repeat our previous mistakes in Afghanistan. We went into Afghanistan, originally in the 1980's, with nothing but a Martial, combative, Anti-Soviet agenda. We then quickly left with no Neptunian sensitivity for the victims we left in the wake of that involvement. Who is the real victim and the real victimizer? With a Mars/Neptune square it is always going to take a deep level of soul wisdom to really know for sure.

At the end of the Cold War in 1990, the combative, Martial, militaristic end of our national consciousness had a chance to integrate with a Neptunian, compassionate, healing energy. I am referring to a specific incident related to me by a friend who was a Colonel in the U.S. Army working at the Pentagon. When the Cold War ended he submitted a well thought-out proposal to his superiors to transform the military into a force for peace. He envisioned a re-organization of the Armed Forces, which would maintain military readiness and training, while also making all of that manpower available to provide food, medicine and other humanitarian aid to other nations suffering from poverty, war, and environmental disasters. His proposal was rejected and resulted in such an uncomfortable environment for him that he was forced into early retirement. That proposal was a chance to have Martial strength and power integrated with Neptunian caring and compassion. Unfortunately the Martian element saw that proposal as too threatening. If Mars and Neptune had integrated to allow our incredible well-funded machinery of war to be used as a beneficent, powerful, force for peace, well, who knows where we would have been on September 11?

First We Hate Them Then We Love Them

I mentioned that we have four planets in the Seventh House, house of partnership and relationship. One of those four planets is the Sun. This is what Hilarion says about Sun in the Seventh House:

> From the lesson point of view, this Sun position calls the native to acquire a sense of *proportion* and *balance* in his attitudes toward "the other," i.e. the love partner. On the one hand, there is too strong an emphasis on the *importance* of the partner in one's life, while on the other hand there is a tendency to try to manipulate and control that other so that the native's pre-conceived ideas about how a love partnership should function will come true. Alas, the usual result of such manipulation is the very opposite of the native's desires: it is to drive a wedge of resentment between him and the partner. If he is perceptive, he will realize at last that the partner is a fully independent individual and should be cherished and honored and loved for *what he is*, rather than being coerced into conforming with the native's fantasies of what should be.[5]

This Sun in the Seventh House tendency to try to get the other person, or in this case, the other nation, to live up to our idea as to how the relationship should function, characterizes U.S. foreign relations and explains why we infuriate so many nations. What makes this even more troubling is the fact that this Sun is 'square,' in tension with, Saturn. This square indicates a resentment of any kind of authority or of having to play by the rules. To again quote Hilarion regarding the Sun aspecting Saturn:

> Saturn in aspect to either of the Lights [Sun or Moon], will bring into the life blockages in terms of dealing with authority, with government, with the police, or with any other authority-concept. The purpose of this pattern, both inside and out, is to bring the individual to the point of recognizing that there is value in guidelines, laws and restrictions — that man must play his "games" in accordance with rules, or else the games

cannot exist. The failure to heed this lesson in past lives has led to loss and backsliding in terms of the learning of soul-lessons.[6]

This explains why the U.S. tends to expect everyone we relate to in the world to do as we wish. When the world comes to us with its own expectations, especially with any kind of collective authority, we then resist and resent the incursion. We respond, once again, with our own agenda. Instances of this are the rejection of the 1997 Kyoto Global Warming Treaty, or the 1992 Earth Summit in Rio de Janeiro, where, en route, President George Bush, Sr. said: "...the American way of life is not up for negotiation." This aspect of our character is also evident in our resistance to submit to the authority of a World Court of Justice, or our unwillingness to pay billions of dollars of our unpaid UN dues. We may always believe we have our reasons, but the fact is our ignorance of these negative traits, illustrated by these Astrological factors, seriously impairs our ability to learn and do better in improving our relationship with the rest of the world.

Fortunately there are also some very positive energies available for us in the other two planets influencing our relationships with others. Here are Hilarion's comments for Venus and for Jupiter in the Seventh House:

> Venus in this sector represents all that is beautiful about a true mated love-relationship.....The seventh house is related to the Venus-ruled sign Libra, and therefore the planet of love is very well placed in this segment of a natus.[7]

> When positively aspected in the seventh, Jupiter promises happiness in marriage — what used to be called a "good match".[8]

Another positive factor is that our Mars is 'trine,' in positive aspect, to our natal Moon in Aquarius. From this placement it would seem that when our Martial energies are truly at the service of Aquarian ideals of universal brotherhood we are less likely to fall prey to the negative Martial traits of aggression in relationships and the 'victim/victimizer' program. It is nice to know that we have these positive relationship qualities and potentials as well. Looking at these planets lined up here in the Seventh House of relationship, one can sense a pattern. First we have Mars, aggressivity and conflict. Then we have Venus, 'all that is beautiful about a true mated love-relationship'. I would say that that is the way we do things. First we beat the hell out of our perceived enemies. Then we befriend them. This pattern was apparent in the Civil War, where the North punished the South in the last year of the war. Yet the North then offered generous terms of surrender in order to restore the previous friendship. In World War II we firebombed the German and Japanese civilian populations as their armies crumbled, yet again offered generous support after the war to regain their friendship. After waging an intense ideological, economic, and military 'Cold War' with the Soviet Union, we are now befriending Russia and the other former Soviet Republics. However, it would be better if we didn't have to be aggressive and belligerent with them first.

Of course, the question now is how do we proceed from here? There are some serious Astrological 'exams' on this part of our Astrological 'curriculum' coming up in the years ahead. These we will investigate in Chapter 8.

---

1 *Astrology Plus*, Hilarion, p. 50.
2 Ibid., p. 156.
3 Ibid., pp. 132-133.
4 Weekday, KUOW Radio, January 1, 2002, Seattle, Washington.
5 *Astrology Plus*, pp. 98-99.
6 Ibid., p. 64.
7 Ibid., pp. 125-126.
8 Ibid., p. 137

7

America's Drug Culture

The planet Neptune, through its association with mystical states of consciousness and with realms of dissolved physical boundaries, is also associated with drug usage. In the late 1960's when Pluto was conjuncting the U.S. natal Neptune, there was a seeming explosion of drug usage in this country. In reality, it was many young people switching from the traditional American drug of choice, namely alcohol, for the 'mind-expansive' drugs of marijuana, LSD and other 'psychedelics'. There was a lot of Plutonian death/rebirth transformation of beliefs and consciousness fueled by these 'mind-expanding' experiences.

Pluto, however, is no longer conjuncting our natal Neptune. It is no longer providing a deep transformative relationship to this experience of altering consciousness. Our natal Neptune being square to natal Mars leaves us with tests involving the negative side of Neptune, such as illusion, confusion, and delusion. This is why we are becoming the 'Prozac Nation'. Clearly there are legitimate uses for psychiatric drugs. There are, however, statistics in this country relative to pharmaceutical drug usage which are quite alarming. The statistics involving children are especially alarming. Nearly 6 million American children between the ages of 6 and 18 are taking prescribed mind-altering drugs. Usage of Ritalin or Methylphenidate for Attention Deficit Hyperactivity Disorder among children has risen from one million in 1990 to 4 million in 2000. The U.N.-sponsored International Narcotics Control Board has attacked the United States for overprescribing stimulants such as Ritalin. The U.S. consumes more than 90 per cent of the Ritalin worldwide. I saw a cartoon which was funny and quite sad at the same time. A teacher was standing before her students next to a large poster which read, 'Say No to Drugs!'. The teacher herself was saying "Now has everyone taken their medications?".

It has been remarked that the largest drug cartel in the world is not in Columbia, but among American pharmaceutical companies. Children are being prescribed Ritalin for such symptoms as 'squirms in seat,' 'interrupts or intrudes on others,' or 'is often on the go'. It sounds to me like children with some planets in the 'fire' signs of Aries, Leo, or Sagittarius. The International Narcotics Control Board, or INCB, reported in 1995 that 10 to 12 percent of all boys between the ages of 6 and 14 in the U.S. have been diagnosed with Attention Deficit Disorder and are being treated with Methylphenidate or Ritalin. One in every 30 Americans between ages 5 and 19 has a prescription for the drug. Furthermore, the INCB has reported that Ritalin's pharmacological effects are essentially the same as those of amphetamine and methamphetamine. The abuse of Ritalin can lead to tolerance and severe psychological dependence. Psychotic episodes and violent bizarre behavior have been reported.

The corollary between pharmaceutical drugs and violence among teens is another alarming study. For example, Shawn Cooper, a 15-year-old who fired two shotgun rounds narrowly missing school staff and students, was taking Ritalin. Kip Kinkel, a 15-year-old who murdered his parents, two students, and wounded 22 other students, had been prescribed both Ritalin and Prozac. T.J. Solomon, a 15-year-old who opened fire and wounded six classmates, was being treated with Ritalin for depression. One of the notorious Columbine High School shooters in Littleton, Colorado, Eric Harris, was revealed, after autopsy, to have used the anti-depressant Luvox or Fluvoxomine prior to the shooting spree.

Supporters of the usage of psychiatric mind-altering drugs prescribed to our nation's youth say that the incidence of depression among teen-agers is much greater than is generally recognized. They argue that if they do not receive some kind of help they are much more likely to commit suicide. Indeed, American teens are already twice as likely to commit suicide than in any other Western nation.

I would think that it would be apparent that these statistics are symptoms of a much deeper malaise within American society. A key factor in this dysfunctionality is the difficult square between Neptune and Mars. Mars in Gemini, in difficult aspect, can be mentally critical and over reliant on its own intellect. Neptune, in difficult aspect, can be escapist and try to blur the rough edges of life with television and countless other forms of escapist entertainment or drugs and alcohol. As with all planets in tension with each other, we tend to go from one extreme to the other. Our over-reliance on our clever, analytical intellect leaves us with the 'wounded feeling function' mentioned by author Robert Johnson in Chapter Five in the subsection 'Beyond Romantic Love'.

To many Americans the only apparent release from this obsessive intellectual identification is to blur the rough edges of it with some form of escape. The healthiest way to heal this dichotomy is with the positive side of Neptune, i.e. a genuine Spiritual life. We desperately need the ego-surrendered experience from such practices as deep prayer and meditation rather than our 'blurring the rough edges' escapism.

As far as our children, they are our mirrors. They act out our own denied elements of ourselves which we repress from conscious awareness. The reason we medicate their pain and depression and 'acting out' is because we can't deal with our own pain and depression. Millions of Americans medicate themselves daily with alcohol and television, if not some pharmaceutical or 'illicit' drug.

Our Mars in the Seventh House of relationships can produce aggression and conflict with others. Trying to medicate (Neptunize) Shawn Cooper, Klip Kinkel, T.J. Solomon, and Eric Harris did not spare them from their outbursts of violence (Mars). Clearly there is a much deeper problem within the American Psyche than simply guns or violence on film and TV. With a Neptune/Mars square, these opportunities to experience violence are just another 'quick fix,' or 'drug rush,' to make one feel alive. They make one feel alive in a world which otherwise seems relatively lifeless. A world where there is little to feel passionate about. My prescription would be anything which provides a deep experience of a non-rational presence of soul. I myself have faith that things are going to change soon.

8

WHERE ARE WE GOING FROM HERE?

In the months leading up to the tragic events of September 11, I was telling my clients that I could feel that something was going to happen. Not because of anything that I knew regarding the U.S. birthchart. I had never seen that chart before. It was because I was aware that a Saturn/Pluto opposition was taking place 'in the sky' in 2001. I became distinctly aware of this tension as I observed how it affected my clients as it aspected factors in their Astrological birthcharts. At the same time, I knew that we were collectively experiencing this Saturn/Pluto tension globally. Saturn represents the status quo, material security, authority, structure, and duty. Pluto, God or Goddess of the Underworld represents the process of deep transformation and regeneration which you cannot avoid.

As the summer of 2001 passed, I could psychically feel the build up of tension between these two planets. Their first exact opposition was on August 5, 2001. I said to my clients that I felt that this Saturn, material, security-minded, stock market report mentality was, sooner or later, going to give way to some deeper, more intense, Plutonian energy. When energies are not allowed to express in a conscious and positive way, they manifest in a negative and often more destructive way. The shadow side of Pluto is secrecy, betrayal, treason, overwhelming violence, and terrorism.

I mentioned earlier in this book a previous Saturn/Pluto opposition which occurred during the Great Depression. That opposition coincided with aspects to the Pluto/Mercury opposition within our birthchart which relates to the issues of material wealth and security as discussed in Chapter Four. That was clearly a time when the joint forces of Saturn and Pluto were having a pronounced effect upon the American experience, as well as the World experience. This is another such time.

This current Saturn/Pluto opposition is falling right on the Ascendant/Descendant axis of the U.S. birthchart. Transiting Pluto is conjuncting the Sagittarian Ascendant of the U.S., which represents our self-image. The impact of this Plutonian 'death/rebirth' of how we see ourselves was the subject of Chapter One. What has not yet been discussed is that this Plutonian 'death/rebirth' of how we see our-selves is occurring along with an opposition to Saturn. The opposing Saturn is moving into our Seventh House, the house of relationships. Here I would like to share what Hilarion has said about aspects between Saturn and Pluto in general:

> The meaning of a Saturn/Pluto contact is that of an extremely far-reaching change being required in the individual in this life. It is a change that affects the unconscious sphere deeply. In some manner an attitude, outlook, way of thinking or approach to some area of the life experience must undergo a *radical* alter-ation, one which in almost every case will be forced upon the individual by events or circumstances *beyond his control*. The signs and houses holding the two planets will give an idea of the change that is required. Pluto will usually point to the gen-eral area, while Saturn will describe the means by which the change must come.[1]

Applying Hilarion's instructions we see that Pluto's position will indicate the general area that needs to be changed. In this case that area would be the Sagittarian self-image and personality of the United States which we explored in Chapter One. Furthermore we see that Saturn's position will describe the *means* by which the change must come. In this case the means would be the Seventh House way we relate to other nations, discussed in Chapter Six. Our perception of ourselves will be changed by events happening in our relationship to other nations. This is where the Saturnian force and pressure is bearing upon us. Clearly, this is in relationship to Arab fundamentalist terror-ists as well as other enemies and allies. Events happening in all of these relationships is putting pressure on how we see ourselves at this time.

In November, 2001, there was another exact opposition of Saturn and Pluto. The third and final opposition will be on May 28, 2002. Later in 2002, Saturn will move to make some very tense aspects to key points in the U.S. birthchart. Saturn will be exactly conjunct to our natal Mars on July 2, 2002. It will be exactly square to our natal Neptune on July 10, 2002. As one remembers that our Mars in the Seventh House has 'the tendency to rush into battle when opposed,' and that our Mars being square to our natal Neptune provokes our 'victim/victimizer program, one senses that April to August 2002 could be a very tense period. One may also notice that July 4th falls right between the 'peak dates' of July 2 and 10, 2002. This could serve as cause for concern that some July 4th event would bear the signature of Martial aggression and Neptunian vulnerability or victimhood.

In my opinion, the most volatile period facing the U.S. in the next several years will be from the end of 2003 until the end of 2006. During this period the planet Pluto, that 'great bringer of change' will be in opposition to our natal Mars placement in the Seventh House, which features our tendency to 'rush into battle when opposed'. During the same time period, Pluto will be squaring our natal Neptune, our potential for illusion, confusion, delusion, victimhood and martyrdom. Looking at these impending Plutonian tensions I can't help but feel that 2003-2006 is when the really intense tests and trials will hit.

Pluto's approach will reveal how well we learned our lessons from the latter part of the 1960's. That was the last time that Pluto was bearing down on the same sectors of our psyche. In that late Vietnam War period, however, Pluto was 'squaring' Mars, but only 'conjuncting' Neptune, which is a profound but less tense aspect. In 2003-06, Pluto will be in tension with both Mars and Neptune. Having both of these placements in tense aspect may well cause the insanity and hatred we are subject to in our relationship to the world to rise to a fever pitch. Whatever we did not learn in Pluto's last appearance in the 60's during Vietnam, we will have to face between late 2003 and late 2006.

The positive potential of Pluto's arrival is that it may very well force the death and rebirth of the negative manifestations of Mars and Neptune in our national character. Perhaps we can recognize the limitations of relating to the world through Martian, i.e. military, approaches. Through this Plutonian death/rebirth we will definitely be more connected to the world we live in.

The more that we all can do within ourselves and with our relationships, our communities, and our collective voices, to choose love instead of fear, the better we will be prepared as a Nation to handle these coming tests. Love and fear are the only two choices. The source of all positive emotions is love. The source of all negative emotions, whether hatred, greed, lust, or jealousy, is fear.

Our 'Progressed' Sun

There is a prognostication tool used in Astrology which I have not yet mentioned. This tool or system is called 'Secondary Progressions'. The way that this system works is where you equate the movement of the planets after birth, day by day, as corresponding with a year by year progression of time. The easiest example of this progression of time would be the progression of the Sun. This is because the Sun moves, essentially, one degree per day. So, in this manner, after ten years of time, by 'Secondary Progression,' the movement of the identity of the Sun in the birthchart will have been 10 degrees. In the case of the U.S. birthchart the 'progressed' Sun would have moved from the 14th degree of Cancer to the 24th degree of Cancer. The other planets move at different speeds, but you would still equate ten days of movement after birth with ten years of actual time having passed.

In a class which I took from Liz Greene, noted Astrologer and author, she theorized that the progressions of the planets in our birthchart show the real growth taking place within the psyche. She concluded that the 'transits' of the planets across our birthchart placements show the concrete means by which that growth takes place.

The main progressions that I tend to look at are the Progressed Sun and the Progressed Moon. The Sun represents the movement of the conscious identity while the Moon symbolizes the movement of the unconscious, instinctual identity. When I look at the present positions of the Progressed Sun and Progressed Moon for the U.S., I feel a greater optimism and hope than when I look at the transits.

The Progressed Moon of the U.S. at this time of February, 2002, is about to conjunct our natal Uranus. Soon after it will move into a positive 'trining' aspect with our natal Saturn. These movements illustrate that we now have the potential to unconsciously and instinctually reconnect to our Uranian capacity to liberate ourselves from the status quo, Saturnian ways of looking at life and how we do things. It is like, unconsciously, we know that something has to give. We understand that we cannot keep going on doing things as we have before. This alignment signifies that the Uranian energies active at our birth in 1776 are being unconsciously re-activated.

Adding to that theme of Uranian freedom and liberation is the present position of our Progressed Sun. Since it moves much slower than the Moon the Progressed Sun's position is more significant. The Progressed Moon circles the zodiac in approximately 28 1/2 years, whereas the Progressed Sun does so in 360 years. Our Progressed Sun is within months of conjuncting our natal Moon in Aquarius. This is another aspect which could well connect us with positive energies from our birth heritage. It could connect us with the Aquarian capacity for 'bringing others together into a united group and encouraging love and brotherhood between them'.

The Progressed Sun in our birthchart has never reached this position before. It has taken 226 years to reach this point. It is a kind of Progressed 'New Moon,' a new birth into the Aquarian New Age ideals upon which this country was founded. This is what is really going on deeper within our psyche. The difficult transits and confrontations we are experiencing consciously are provided to enable us to transform and open to this new birth. Hopefully, once and for all we can accept the role which this country was meant to play in relation to the World's family of Nations.

Additional Positive Transits

In 2005, Saturn will be moving into a positive, 'sextiling' transit to our natal Neptune, situated in the Ninth House realm of philosophy and religion. As discussed earlier, Neptune placed here gives us the capacity for either true mystical faith and surrender, or for illusion and confusion. Saturn's 'sextiling' transit of that Neptune will be grounding, making 'real' the need to accept Neptune's positive qualities into our lives. Without true spirituality and faith this material world is nothing but a 'crap shoot'.

Acknowledging our spiritual hunger has been sidetracked by our tendency to experience Neptune in an either/or manner, due to our birthchart 'square' between Neptune and Mars. Either you can have Neptunian spirituality, or you can have Mars in Gemini intelligence. It is difficult to have both with such tension. This situation has allowed the meaningful discussion of God and Spirit on our lives to be overshadowed by the Fundamentalist Religious Right, or to be pushed to the fringes of the New Age. Maybe by 2005, when the grounding quality of the planet Saturn starts to move into positive aspect with this Neptune, we will start to own and integrate our birthchart capacity to truly embody spirituality in the way we view life and in the way we live life.

At the same time that 'transiting' Saturn will be making this positive aspect to our natal Neptune in 2005, 'transiting' Neptune in the sky will be making a positive aspect, by 'trine,' to our natal Saturn. These reflexive, simultaneous transits involving the same two planets will reinforce the force and function of each one. The Neptune 'trine' to natal Saturn will affect our Saturn's Tenth House 'role in the world'. Hilarion's comments on the Tenth House Saturn revealed the need to 'put considerable effort into his job or career' to overcome 'habits of sloth and inattention'. With this Neptune transit there will be the potential to open to and align our sense of 'job or career' with true compassion, healing, and spirituality. This 'transit' will take place during and in the wake of whatever events are forced upon us by the intense Plutonian transits active between 2003 and 2006. As Pluto bears down upon our potential for Martial militaristic aggression and Neptunian delusion, this Neptune transit will help open our hearts and our souls.

How Do We Go From Here?

All the world is watching us now. How we handle ourselves and our relations around the world is critical to the entire planet at this time. As I have pointed out the negative traits within the American character, I have realized that I, as an American, have some of these same traits. I share tendencies towards Sagittarian self-righteousness, Mars in Gemini criticalness, and lessons to be learned around sexuality. What can I do as an individual to reconcile these issues? What can we do as a Nation? We can step by step confess, admit our failings, acknowledge our faults, ask to be forgiven, forgive ourselves, and then promise to try to do better.

When I first received the Hilarion Astrological material it was about a month after my divorce. It was a time when I was already having to be honest with myself. When I read the Hilarion pronouncements regarding my own birthchart, I felt as if I were 'nailed to the cross,' as it were. It forced me to acknowledge that these were indeed my lessons. I promised to try to do better, and to stop blaming life or other people for my mistakes. They became easier to accept when Hilarion's teaching helped me realize that the feeling of guilt is a fairly useless emotion. Hilarion says that once there is the awareness that a mistake has been made, to continue to feel guilty about it inhibits your capacity to make the changes which would be required so that you no longer make that mistake.

As I have written this analysis of the American experience I have, at times, felt a bit over-critical. I think that a lot of that stems from frustration with the way life is now being lived in comparison to how it could be. In the 1960's, when Pluto was conjuncting our natal Neptune, for many of us there was a spiritual revolution going on. Pluto, the planet of complete transformation, was bearing down upon our Neptune. That brought the Plutonian capacity for 'death and rebirth' into contact with our capacity for spiritual faith and surrender.

In the summer of 1969 when I was 17 years old, I went to the Woodstock Music Festival in upstate New York. I arrived two weeks before it started. My personal experience at Woodstock was so profound, I thought this was going to change the world. What I saw there was the power of love. Love was the glue that allowed four or five hippies from every small town on the East Coast to join with many more from the cities, until over 500,000 people came together to celebrate this new consciousness.

Woodstock's last performance was on Monday morning, for those of us still there. It was Jimi Hendrix. When he played 'The Star Spangled Banner' with so much exuberance, many of us cried. We cried with a hope and a faith that the love and universally acknowledged brother/sisterhood which all of us embodied spiritual souls carry in our deepest heartfelt longing could actually happen. That it could actually come true. Immediately after Woodstock, however, the mainstream media moved in and the movement lost its innocence. Many of us eventually settled for a certain kind of complacency. The seeds of that time have continued growing here and there, sprouting in other areas of emerging consciousness. But the visions of a truly transformed world I experienced at Woodstock never really manifested. At least not yet. I keep hoping. I've tried hard to do my own small part to keep that hope alive. There are resonant enclaves of the spirit of those times here and there. I still have faith in this country.

I don't think we are as evil or vain as the rest of the world tends to think. We are just ignorant, or asleep, or complacent. As a result, we have a distorted view of the world and how to relate to it. Our misconceptions have inhibited us from surrendering to love as a nation and sharing it with the world. In Hilarion's book 'Nations' he discusses this American dilemma and the 'terrible years ahead.' The exact nature of what that entails will be discussed in the last chapter:

> This great country must have its rebirth along with all the rest. In many ways she is the greatest nation the earth has ever known. But she is flawed today by a blindness which has crept into her perception of the world. In the terrible years ahead,

although she herself will be preserved almost to the end from the full onslaught, she will see with increasing alarm the destruction and the loss which the baser passions of man will bring.

At last, in an agony of the soul, America will again stand forth with her love, to rescue and nurture the peoples of the world whose nations have collapsed and disintegrated in the terrors that man has brought upon himself. By that act she will again and for all time be purified. In the new age that will dawn for mankind, America will lead the world as a great and burning beacon of truth, of justice, of peace and of purity.[2]

All I can say is: Amen.

---

1   *Astrology Plus*, Hilarion, p. 66.
2   *Nations*, Hilarion, p. 23.

9

A Tarot Reading For the United States

The following is an account of a 'Celtic Cross' Tarot Card Reading which I performed on the evening of September 12, 2001, for the United States of America, in respect of the previous day's events.

There were ten cards presented in this reading. These ten cards represented: 1. The past, 2. The recent past, what had just recently passed away, 3. The present, 4. The unconscious energies being experienced at that time, 5. The conscious energies being experienced at that time, 6. Our present experience of ourselves, 7. The effect or influence of individuals or factors external to the U.S. upon the U.S., 8. Our hopes or fears, or possibly both, 9. The possible next phase, and 10. The possible overall outcome of this particular cycle of events.

These were the ten cards in the reading:

1. **The Past - Princess of Disks**

2. **The Recent Past - Queen of Disks**

3. **The Present - Nine of Wands - Strength**

4. **The Unconscious Energies - Ace of Wands.**

5. **The Conscious Energies - Seven of Swords - Futility**

6. **Our Experience of Ourselves - The Wheel of Fortune**

7. **The Influence or Effect of People or Factors in Our Outer Environment Upon Us: Knight of Wands**

8. **Our Hopes or Fears - The Priestess**

9. **The Possible Next Phase - Seven of Disks - Failure**

10. **Possible outcome of this cycle of Events - (to be revealed at the end)**

The Past is the **Princess of Disks**. She has a staff with a diamond on its tip. The diamond is the brightest, most valuable gemstone, but the only way that a diamond can come into being is to take a mineral and place it under the heaviest earth pressure, for the longest period of time. I think this relates to our country during and after Vietnam. This was when we were feeling various pressures, and were questioning ourselves and what we truly stood for.

The Recent Past - The Queen of Disks. She is very grounded and practical. She is a positive, steady worker, but her work can become a drudgery rather than an inspiration. I would say that this describes where we have been since the early eighties, a bit overly obsessed with materialistic concerns.

The Present - Nine of Wands - Strength. If nothing else, the horrific events of September 11 have made us invoke our strength, passion, and will as a nation.

The Unconscious Energies - Ace of Wands. This is an outrush of will energy in its most dynamic form. This is resonant with the previous card. The energies of passion and will are aroused to the maximum within our unconscious.

The Conscious Energies - Seven of Swords - Futility. Despite the fire and the will and the passion, we are still mentally uncertain, unclear and hesitant. We don't know what we are going to do, what they are going to do, and what is really going on here.

Our Experience of Ourselves - The Wheel of Fortune. The experience of this card occurs after you have been around and around, up and down, for so many times that you have finally gained the ability to go to the center of the wheel. From that center you can see the ups and downs of your life with objectivity and detached clarity. I do see us stepping a bit 'out of the movie' of our lives and trying to get some clarity on what is going on here. These events were just too big, too Plutonian, for us to just carry on as usual.

The Effect or Influence of Factors in Our Outer Environment Upon Us - Knight of Wands. This Knight is the lower or negative aspect of the sign Sagittarius, which includes fanaticism. The Knight of Wands, in my system, is very noble, very courageous, and has great fiery and willful aspiration. However, he is based on fear, to the extent that he is very impulsive. He receives an inspiration and then charges off, until he uses up all of his energy and collapses. As soon as he revives then he is off again. He is kind of manic-depressive. This is easy to recognize in the character and behavior of the 9/11 terrorists. The card in this position, however, also represents the possible reaction within us, because of our having to deal with the manic-depressive energy outside of ourselves. Basically, we could become noble and courageous, yet impulsive, if we choose to respond out of fear and not out of wisdom.

Our Hope or Fear- The Priestess. This card corresponds to the Moon. She is the Goddess of the Moon, the perfect reception and reflection of the spiritual light. The Priestess is a being of great purity and sensitivity. This card represents both our hope of attaining this state of spiritual purity and sensitivity, as well as our fear that we will start down a path from which we may never get back to this possibility for ourselves.

The Possible Next Phase: Seven of Disks - Failure. This card corresponds to Saturn in Taurus. The time of Taurus is largely during the month of May, when the leaves are green, the flowers are blooming, the birds are singing, and everyone is in love. The planet Saturn represents karma, testing, and lessons. Here Saturn has come into the month of May, and has turned all of the leaves black, dead and dying. The reason there is a sense of failure is because the potential for the month of May isn't being fully lived or realized. It looks like this sense of strength we have now isn't going to last. The opportunity for the month of May will feel limited and restricted.

The Possible Outcome of this Particular Cycle of Events - The Devil. The Devil is actually a good card, despite its associations in Christianity. It is one of the so-called 'major arcana' cards, like the Fool, the Magician, The Emperor, etc. Each of these cards symbolize necessary initiations, some being more pleasant than others. The initiation of the Devil requires that you must face your own Devil, that which blocks or limits you from being who you really are and can be. These limits are the illusions that have been laid onto you or that you have willingly accepted, even though they are not really true. It is only your belief in these illusions which give them power over you. The reason that the Devil is a good card is that until you can see your Devil, or limits, you can't do anything to get past it. This initiation is where you have to face the music. It looks like we Americans will take a long hard look at ourselves to see what is real and what isn't. What events it will take to eventually bring us to that point is the pressing question.

10

THE ARAB/ISRAELI CONFLICT AND THE TRIBULATION

The original inspiration to present the material in this book was the terrorist attacks on September 11, 2001. In the Astrological analysis I have put forth, I have pointed at flaws in the American experience of itself which could lead to our vulnerability to serving as a target for such hatred. A major underlying source of tension between the U.S. and the Muslim extremists, however, is the unlimited U.S. support for Israel.

Hilarion has given specific information regarding Israel and the over-all Arab/Israeli conflict. In the book *The Nature of Reality: A Book of Explanations*, Hilarion predicts there will be a period of severe testing and trial of the race of humanity called the Tribulation. He describes it as 'a season of sorrow and shock for the race.' The predictions for humanity were quite dire when they were made in that 1979 book. Since then, Hilarion has said that conditions on earth have changed and it is far less likely that those events will take place in the extreme degree in which they were originally portrayed. He says that the possibilities are always in a state of flux. But to make no mistake, there will be a period of severe testing and trial of the race of humanity on this planet.

The following is my own synopsis of the basic principles of the Tribulation. I recommend the Hilarion Series of books for much more detailed information. Hilarion says that the Tribulation was set in motion some 12,000 years ago, during the destruction of Atlantis. At that time, it was realized that mankind was not on pace to reach the basic goal of freedom from the wheel of rebirth within the amount of time allotted to us. We only have so much time to accomplish this. That is because the Earth, herself, is a conscious being, and is now ready to ascend to a higher level of vibration to begin her next phase of evolution. If she were to do that at this time, however, many individuals on the Earth would find those higher vibratory energies extremely uncomfortable or they would use them for very negative, destructive purposes. And so the Tribulation is a necessary period of trial and cleansing for humanity. Native American Hopi's have called it 'The Great Purification' in their prophecies. It is not a time of punishment, as in a Fundamentalist Christian sense, but instead a time of final encouragement to people to change before it is too late.

My understanding is that the real tragedy at this time is not if you lose your physical body. It is if you lose your soul. If you lose your body, if you die physically during this time period but you are of the more evolved segment of humanity, you will be able to reincarnate back into the on-going human evolution on this planet. However, if you do not, at some point during the Tribulation, open to a faith in something beyond your own ego, and to a willingness to live in peace with your brothers and sisters on this planet, then you will have lost your opportunity to continue with the human family on this planet. You will be removed to a separate sphere of darkness. Hilarion says that it is a huge tragedy to lose even one soul because it has taken us billions of years for us to arrive at this stage of evolution.

There are three main groups or segments of humanity now, according to Hilarion. One group is composed of those who are already of the Light, who know in their hearts how life could be on this planet if we were willing to live in peace and love. To these people, Hilarion says that they need have no fear. They can have faith that they will be guided when and to where they need to be, when they need to be there. These individuals simply need to be willing to serve, in whatever way they are capable. There is a second group of humanity which Hilarion describes as being almost hopelessly lost in darkness. He says there is almost nothing that can be done to save them. There is then a third group which in fact is the largest. This is made up of the many people who can go either way, towards the light or the darkness. Hilarion says it is this middle group which the Spiritual Hierarchy are most concerned about.

Hilarion points out that there is a large black etheric cloud around this planet, created by all of the hatred, greed, and other negative emotions emanating from its inhabitants. This black cloud greatly limits our ability to open and further evolve our consciousness. The only way to disperse this cloud is to either transmute it through the opposite emotions of love and compassion, or by allowing this etheric vibrational negativity to physically manifest into war and destruction on the earth. Those in the higher planes concerned with our evolution are allowing us as much time as possible to transform this dark cloud through the first means. However, we only have so much time. Hilarion has also said that humanity, of its own free will, can set the Tribulation in motion at any time.

The Arab/Israeli Conflict

According to Hilarion, the Middle East is the place to watch. He says that the oil deposits which ring the State of Israel were purposely arranged to be there to serve as the catalyst for what Hilarion calls the *casus belli* for the final war. The Spiritual Hierarchy understood that the nations of the Earth would fight for ownership of the oil deposits. I must admit that during the Gulf War I thought, 'This is it.'

In the book, Nations, Hilarion has a specific pronouncement regarding Israel. Before I present that information, I would like to share some Astrological insight into the Arab/Israeli conflict. In his book, *Alan Oken's Complete Astrology*, the author contends that Astrologically speaking the Israelis are related to the sign Aries while the Arabs are related to the sign Scorpio. Aries and Scorpio are the two signs which are ruled by Mars, the God of War. This gives insight into why both sides exhibit seemingly irrepressible, aggressive, and violent tendencies. However, the Aries and Scorpio 'styles' are totally different. The Aries related Israelis express their aggression in blustering 'Six Days Wars' campaigns with helicopter gunships and tanks. In contrast, the Scorpio related Arabs express their aggression in smaller secretive, terrorist attacks and suicide bombers. Each side totally hates and resents the other's 'style.'

I have traveled to Israel. I made a spiritual pilgrimage to Jerusalem, as a Christian. I also made a pilgrimage to the northern Israeli town of Zefat, as a devoted student of the Jewish Kabbalah. In the 16th century there was a great flowering of Kabbalistic teaching and knowledge in Zefat. The hillside there is dotted with numerous gravesites, many painted blue to indicate the resting place of a *tzadikim* or holy person.

While in Israel I also visited with Israeli friends. These were largely European Jews, friends and family of my Jewish friends in Europe. They told me that, at one time, they had great hope and faith in the future of their country. During the 1960's and 70's there was a lot of positive optimism for the future of their nation. That was the time when a lot of *kibbutzim* and other communal efforts flourished. My friends then told me that their optimism is gone. They have little faith in their future. I was told this in 1987, long before the present *intifada*.

At that same time, these friends of European descent also told me that the most aggressive, anti-Palestinian, and militant Israelis tended to be Jews who came from Arabic countries such as Morocco and Yemen. These Jews already had developed a long history of tension with Muslims. My friends noted that the other group of Israelis who were equally aggressive and militaristic in their attitude toward the Palestinians were Jews who had emigrated from America.

Here, I am venturing onto tricky ground, in relation to my many Jewish-American friends. Nonetheless, I say what I say now because it is my observation, and I offer it only to further awareness and consciousness and healing. My Jewish-American friends are generally very liberal, abhor racial discrimination, and are firm advocates of Civil Rights. Yet among many of them, once the subject of Israel is mentioned, a whole different demeanor descends over them. They become aggressive and militaristic in their attitude towards the Palestinians. Of course the sad history of anti-Semitism and the horrors of the Holocaust are a large and understandable cause for Jewish protectiveness. However, why would American Jews be more militant in their defense of Israel than European Jews, who are actually more connected to the historical areas where those horrors took place? My conclusion is that the American Jews are likely subject to the elements of the American Astrological character. These Astrological influences would include the Sagittarian Ascendant tendency to see oneself as 'upright, honest and morally strong, *whether true or not*'; the Mars in the Seventh House 'tendency to rush into battle when opposed'; and the Neptune/Mars square leading to the 'victim/victimizer program.' These are all American birthchart characteristics which could lead American Jews to dismiss or downplay Israelis who support peace and a less aggressive approach to the Israeli/Palestinian conflict.

Before I quote Hilarion's comments on Israel, I would like to repeat what Hilarion has said regarding prophecy. He stated that the best prophet was the *false prophet*, he whose prophecy has failed to come true. By delivering his prophecy he has encouraged people to change sufficiently so that the prophecy no longer needs to occur. The material for the book *Nations* was originally channeled from Hilarion in 1979. Much has changed in the fate of nations since that time. For example, the information regarding Iran references 1979 when the Ayatolloh Khomeini seized power. Hilarion's predictions for Iran then were quite dire, but the possibilities are always in flux. Today with reformist forces gaining political power there is cause for greater hope in Iran. People and nations always have the opportunity to change and thus alter their destiny. Here are Hilarion's comments on Israel:

ISRAEL has lost her Master.

She has forgotten the god who guided her people through the long centuries of affliction and persecution. Because she has forgotten her god, she will be tested in the very center of the crucible when the bitter years are upon the earth. This trial will bring the nation back to god, but only after much has been suffered.

Israel has been the repository of a burning faith and devotion for many centuries. She was meant to carry that flame aloft so that in the Tribulation years new fires could be lighted from it, to bring the world back to a true faith.

Those of her people who remained in other countries have still that intensity of dedication to their religion which can fulfill the stated purpose during the Last Days. But among the people of the new state of Israel there is only a mockery of faith. They do not believe any more. And because of their unbelief they will be forced to drink the bitter cup to the dregs in the years of trouble ahead.[1]

Hilarion's observations on Israel echo the lack of faith admitted by my Israeli friends. In reading Hilarion's *Nations*, it is clear that it is no accident what nation you are born into, or choose to live in. It is also clear that the Tribulation is going to come down more forcefully in certain parts of the planet than in others. Historians have looked back to World War II and we can now see clearly what could have been done by various nations to avoid or lessen the horrors that ensued. If and when the Middle East conflagration fully ignites, historians will look back at the role which the U.S. played in that eruption, both in terms of what we did and didn't do. Personally, I think that the many flaws in the American character are leading us to fail to live up to what this country does and should truly stand for. In addition to the flaws of Sagittarian self-righteousness and Martial aggression, there is our Saturnian Tenth House 'sloth and inattention' in relation to our role in the world. This negligent attitude coupled with our Saturn square Sun's resentment of any kind of authority, explains why we do not support the only body of authority which could bring peace to the Middle East. The U.S. is the key player in denying that body of authority its true potential role and mission. That body would be of course, a fully empowered and functioning United Nations. In an interview with Retired Rear Admiral Eugene Carroll relative to non-military solutions to conflict in the world were the following comments:

Admiral Carroll: We had leaders who helped found the United Nations and make it reflect our objectives, interests and values. The Charter is an American document and yet we have been among the least supportive in the last 50 years of any nation in the world.

Weekday host: If there was one thing you could do, if you could wave your magic wand to make the United Nations stronger, what would it be?

Admiral Carroll: The U.S. taking it more seriously, its responsibility seriously, paying its dues and supporting the changes in the U.N. which are absolutely essential to make it effective as an institution.

Weekday: But it still has hope for you as an institution?

Admiral Carroll: I know of no other game in town that has any promise whatever. The Charter is magnificent. It has all of the authority in writing that it needs. It doesn't have the support and leadership of the United States to translate the authority into capabilities.[2]

It was dismaying to me when I learned that a proposal to put U.N. peace monitors on the Israel/Palestine border had been accepted by the entire body of U.N. nations, except for two—the U.S. and Israel. Of course, the U.S. exercised its Security Council veto and the proposal was killed.

I am happy to read in Hilarion's *Nations* that "in an agony of soul, America will again stand forth with her love, to rescue and nurture the peoples of the world". How long it takes for the present 'blindness' to be removed will determine how much good we can do. It will also determine how much guilt we must carry, collectively, for what we could have done if we had awakened sooner. It is partly with that in mind that I am writing this book.

The Experiment Of Oceania

Hilarion says that there is a unique experiment taking place on this one planet within the entire Universe. He says that the other galactic races refer to this planet as 'Oceania.' This is because virtually nowhere in the Universe is there a planet with this much water. He says that on other planets that have water at all, it is like a pond with a fence around it. But virtually nowhere is there the vast oceans as on this planet. These oceans have been placed on this planet, says Hilarion, to advance the unique experiment unfolding on Earth.

Hilarion instructs that there are three main facets to the Godhead: mental, emotional, and physical. He says that the other galactic races, which are generally much more evolved than us, are evolving along the 'mental ray.' They have learned to live in peace with each other because they mentally understand the Karmic Law. 'As you sow so shall you reap.' Whereas, we have been given the much more difficult task of evolving along the 'emotional ray.' That is why there is so much water here, to create an emotional atmosphere. The other galactic races have had little faith that we would succeed. That is because our path requires that we be subject to the entire range of emotional experience, including hatred, greed, and violence. However, the hope is that we can come to the place where we live in peace and no longer harm others, not only because we mentally understand the Karmic Law, but because we have embraced Love.

In this light, I would like to end this book with Hilarion's closing comments in the 1990 revised edition of *The Nature of Reality*:

> And remember that earth humanity has volunteered to show the rest of the universe what love can do. For the most part, other cosmic races have chosen the mental path, and do not understand what good can come of unchaining the emotional nature — particularly as they observe the sorrow and destruction that humans on this planet have fashioned from the excesses of their negative emotions. But these same emotions will be purified, and once cleansed of the dross of self, they will become wings that speed the soul towards a glory that even the most wildly optimistic among you has not yet dared to imagine.

May the peace and blessing of all the higher beings who care for humanity's struggle be with you forevermore.

OM MANI PADME HUM

1   *Nations*, Hilarion, p. 17.
2   Weekday, KUOW Radio, January 1, 2002, Seattle, Washington

Supplemental
Chapters
to the
Second Edition

11

UPDATE TO THE 2ND EDITION

Since writing the first edition of this book I have observed numerous ways in which the Astrological karma of the U.S.A. continues to manifest. Although we Americans continue to ignore many of our lessons, I am feeling hopeful, even optimistic. The Sufi sect of mystical Islam asserts that sometimes you have to go down into grief and suffering before you can go up. The psychologist Carl Jung once said that there is no growth without pain and suffering.

In the first edition of this book I predicted that particularly strong tests and lessons would bear down on the American experience of itself from the end of 2003 until the end of 2006. As Pluto transits the sky, moving through our First house of self-image, this planet which brings major transformations has been coming into tension with the Mars/Neptune square in our natal chart. The last time that Pluto activated this Mars/Neptune square was during the Vietnam War. It is clearly no accident that many resonances and references to the cauldron of the Vietnam experience are manifesting now. Magazine covers I saw back in 2003 while traveling in Europe have frequently displayed the question: 'Iraq, The New Vietnam?'. More recently Newsweek magazine has finally put the Vietnam comparison on their front cover.

It is also no accident that Erroll Morris' brilliant documentary about former Secretary of Defense Robert McNamara's reflections on past U.S. military involvements, particularly Vietnam, won the Oscar for Best Documentary at the 2004 Academy Awards. The title of the film couldn't be a more applicable metaphor for a Neptunian brew of watery, confusion, and delusion, coming into tension with a Martial penchant to 'rush into battle when opposed,' thus coalescing as, 'The Fog of War.'

McNamara confesses that part of the U.S. justification for engaging in the conflict in Vietnam was fabricated. The alleged North Vietnamese attack on a US naval vessel in the 'Gulf of Tonkin' incident has been revealed as a fraud designed to inflame America's public opinion. McNamara's admission now appears in our national experience at the same time that fabrications and manipulations of U.S. intelligence used to validate the 2003 invasion of Iraq are coming to light. It is, again, no accident that these parallels with Vietnam continue to manifest.

When I wrote the first edition of this book, the U.S. was primarily focused on its military engagement in Afghanistan. When war with Iraq later seemed imminent, I feared that with these Vietnam era Astrological transits recurring, the U.S. could repeat the Vietnam debacle of forty years before. If we sought to quell terrorism with exclusively Mars, i.e. military methods, then invasion of Iraq would descend into a Neptunian vulnerable swamp of confusion, illusion, and victimhood.

A recent example of a manifestation of this Mars/Neptune aggression coupled with victimhood are the recent prisoner abuse scandals perpetrated by American Military personnel. A recent International Red Cross report alleges that abuse of Iraqi prisoners by American soldiers was broad and represented a pattern tolerated by coalition forces, not just 'individual acts.' Some of the abuses were tantamount to torture involving brutality, humiliation and threats of imminent execution. I would say that the last time the American public had to witness this American Mars/Neptune aggression and victimization on their daily television was during the Vietnam War.

I have also seen another manifestation of this rather intense Astrological karma facing the U.S. experience of ourselves at this time. Our natal Mars is in the Seventh House, the house of partnership and relationship to others. This would include our relationships with nations supporting the U.S. as partners as well as with those nations with whom we may have conflict. Readers may note that partnering with the U.S. at this time, in our Martial/military endeavors may make other nations subject to their own Martial/Plutonian destruction and Neptunian cycle of victimhood and martyrdom. Such partnering has resulted in the bombing of British targets in Turkey while George Bush was visiting British Prime Minister Tony Blair in London. And more recently the train bombings in Madrid have severely damaged our support and military partnership with Spain.

In the light of all of the above one may ask how I can feel optimistic and hopeful. The horror of Vietnam forced many Americans to look more deeply into what our government was doing and into who we are and who we want to be. I now see a similar kind of introspection that is taking place within our nation today.

Frankly, when I saw this 2003-2006 Pluto transit approaching, I expected that the U.S. would be involved in even greater conflict. I now sense that the upcoming 2004 election and the choices it represents is a major part of the manifestation of Pluto bearing down on our Mars/Neptune tension. This fundamental tension between Martial power and Neptunian compassion is exacerbated by the Plutonian pressure of life or death urgency. This is reflected in the passion with which the Republicans and the Democrats attack each other from opposite sides of this dynamic tension . Those emphasizing Mars, generally Republicans, feel that if we don't act in a predominantly Martial, aggressive military manner, then we will be Neptunian victims. Those emphasizing a greater influence of Neptune, generally Democrats, feel that if we don't demonstrate enough Neptunian sensitivity and compassion to others, then we will elicit Martial/militaristic responses to our actions resulting in victimhood and martyrdom

Balanced integration of these opposing perspectives would help us reconcile our national goals and integrate the tense dynamics in our Astrological birthchart. Although the fall of Saddam Hussein may have benefitted the Iraqi people, I agree with my European brothers and sisters who say this was the wrong war at the wrong time for the wrong reasons. The purpose of Pluto, moving through our First House of Self-image bearing down upon this Martial/Neptunian karma, is for us to examine ourselves. It is an opportunity to look deeply into where we are really coming from. What is it that truly motivates us? Is it love and generosity of heart or is it fear, greed, and selfishness? Again, many Americans are using this Plutonian intensity to look deeper into what truly inspires each of us and those who purport to lead this country.

Instead of capitalizing on this Plutonian introspection, however, George Bush and the cabal surrounding him, seek to usurp Pluto's power. They are trying to dominate, manipulate and even annihilate all their perceived enemies with a Plutonian obsession, eschewing any moral self-questioning. Astrologer Robert Hand explains the possible negative effects of Pluto transiting the First House:

> Now you have the chance to be either a positive or a negative force for change in the world around you, but you will almost certainly be a negative force if you don't make the effort to understand yourself. You will be the vehicle for blind and irrational ego forces, the result of infantile and primitive urges that you haven't dealt with as an adult.[1]

The American media is replete with news of the recently blatant manifestations of these blind and irrational forces surging up from our national psyche. It is not a good idea, however, to try to take over the power of a God. Greek tragedy is littered with the unfortunate destinies of such hubris, especially a God such as Pluto.

Again, why am I optimistic? For one, I am optimistically hoping that Bush is going to lose the 2004 election. I think that Kerry could be the leader to bring us back from the brink. John Kerry has the ability to bring some balance and integration to the Martial/Neptunian tension in our national experience. In 2005 and 2006 these intense Plutonian transits to Mars and Neptune will continue to make exact 'hits' on our natal chart. So whoever is President is likely to have to deal with some major challenges over the next two years. If America chooses four more years of George W. Bush, that would scare me with these transits happening. Even if that is the case, however, I would trust that that must be what the U.S. needs for its own growth and evolution. As I said before, sometimes you have to go down before you can go up.

1 *Planets in Transit*, Robert Hand, p. 478.

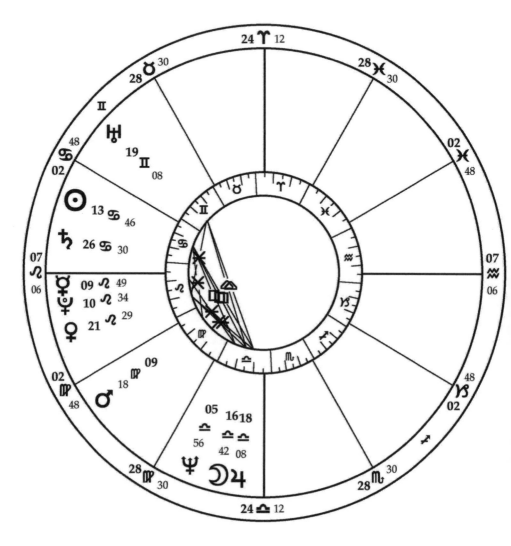

George W. Bush

Natal Chart
Saturday, July 6, 1946
7:26:00 AM EDT
New Haven, Connecticut
Tropical   Porphyry   True Node

12

THE ASTROLOGICAL KARMA OF
GEORGE W. BUSH

President George W. Bush, perhaps more than any other in recent history, has polarized our nation into nearly 50/50 opposed camps. Those who approve of George W. Bush and all or most of what he has done and those who approve of little or nothing of what he has done. This polarity in the national psyche reflects what the U.S. is experiencing now in its own Astrological birthchart as a nation. Examination of Bush's Astrological birthchart reveals that he and our nation are both confronting similar challenges by identifying with our self image at the expense of our true natures.

In this discussion of the Astrological birthchart of George W. Bush I will first look at him as an individual. Behind the social persona of every individual there is a matrix of factors which influence the choices and decisions we each make in the performance of our social obligations. The Astrological factors evident in the birthchart and reflected in the formative experiences in his childhood and later life give a more comprehensive view of this man. I will then review the influence of these factors and others on how George W. Bush functions as President and conclude with the dangers I see ahead for George W. Bush and our nation.

George W. Bush is a Cancer. He thinks he is a Leo. He pretends that he is an Aries. In his childhood he had to bear the influence of the sign Libra. All in a manner of speaking. These are prominent basic Astrological influences in the drama of George W. Bush's life

As stated earlier, the Sun in a birthchart represents your soul essence. It is who you really are. George Bush has his Sun in Cancer, born on July 6 two days after our own U.S. birthday of July 4th. This means that the soul essence of George W. Bush has developed qualities of caring and nurturing in previous lives. He would be a a good man to represent 'family values' and a traditional, patriotic stance. It is this Cancerian part of George Bush which would resonate sincerely with his stated mission of 'compassionate conservatism.'

I previously explained that the United States is not always in touch with the caring, nurturing potential of its Sun in Cancer. Our nation often tends to identify more with our self-righteous Sagittarian self-image. Similarly, George W. Bush's Sun in Cancer qualities of caring and nurturing are often overwhelmed by the smug superiority of his self image (Ascendant) which is Leo.

This sign as well as the Sign Aries, his projected image to the world (Midheaven), are both feisty fire signs. Aries on the Midheaven will show a tendency to present oneself as 'headstrong, willful and dynamic', with a tendency to appear as 'hot-headed.'

The self image of Bush is better understood by analyzing Hilarion's description of Leo Ascendant:

> When the sign Leo rises, there will be a tendency for the self-picture to be colored by the notions of elegance, specialness and superiority. A proudness will often be felt internally.... The reason for giving this Ascendant to an individual is to prompt him to think better of himself than he is in the habit of doing when in incarnation. The rulership by the sun thus lends to the individual certain bolstering influences in terms of how he sees himself, which are intended to teach him not to underestimate his own worth and not to feel inferior to others.[1]

So, the Leo Ascendant is given to an individual to bolster their self-esteem as a counterforce to their own self-doubt. Thus George W. Bush's self image protects him against feeling inferior to others so as to appear stronger than he is.

In addition to the Leo Ascendant, Bush has Mercury in Leo in the First House close to the Ascendant, of which Hilarion says:

Mercury here [in Leo]......will aggravate feelings of pride, superiority and arrogance. The thoughts will revolve ever and only about the self, and the person's life will seem to him to be a magnificent play in which he himself is the main actor, and has written all the parts. The main lesson is to *see others as whole persons in their own right*, living their own life-plays.[2]

This Mercury is conjunct to Pluto in Bush's chart, which indicates that the soul's tendencies for arrogance and self-absorption have been slated for major transformation in this life. The dichotomy between a caring, nurturing father and an arrogant, smirking, party boy is a basic theme duly noted in all of the biographies I have read about George W. Bush. In his own auto-biography, 'A Charge to Keep,' Bush speaks in great detail about the reasons why he refused to commute the death sentence of Karla Faye Tucker, a reformed murderer turned Christian who had asked for the right to live so that she could aid and counsel other young women in prison who had also been led down the path of drugs and violence. She had appeals on her behalf coming from sources all the way up to Pope John Paul himself.

George Bush explained that he did not commute the death sentence of Karla Fay Tucker, while at the same time he did commute the death sentence of an unrepentant serial killer, Henry Lee Lucas, because facts revealed that Lucas was innocent in relation to the specific murder he was convicted of, whereas Karla Faye Tucker had never professed innocence for what she did. He admits being heavy of heart at the time. Indeed, his wife Laura said that she had never seen George so anxious and that he was having difficulty falling asleep. After the execution, however, a journalist asked Bush what Karla Faye's response had been when CNN's Larry King had asked her what she would say to Governor Bush if she had the opportunity. Bush mocked and mimicked Karla Faye by saying, 'Please don't kill me,' in a whimpering voice.[3]

Which of these reactions is more truthful? That reported by Laura Bush, or that by the journalist? Admittedly, George W. thought that his comments with the journalist were off the record. I believe that Bush's caring, emotional, Cancerian Self was sincerely tortured by the death of Karla Fay Tucker on his hands. His inability to access, own, and consistently express that caring emotional side, however, is a major dilemma for him in this life. This is the same dilemma faced by this great nation of ours.

Personally, I see George W. Bush as a rather wounded Cancer. I say this not only because of the dichotomy between his Leo Ascendant/Aries Midheaven and his Cancer Sun, but because all the tension in his chart (three squares) is afflicting his Sun in Cancer. The themes involved in this tension relate to experiences in childhood, his own past life memory, the family unconscious, and the quality of his mind and belief system.

George W. has the Moon, which represents childhood, in positive aspect to his Venus. This indicates that there was a lot of love and affection in his childhood. This aspect coincides with a close emotional relationship with the mother, which, in George W.'s case by all accounts seems to be true. His Moon is also conjunct to Jupiter, which would represent a positive, beneficent, fortunate, expansive influence in his childhood. The wealth, affluence, and prestige attained by his father, the large family, and the warm-hearted outspokenness of his mother, would all point to this positive influence of Jupiter.

There is a complex of Astrological factors here, however, which would show additional influences at work in the childhood and psychological make-up of George W. Bush. Before I explain these factors, however, I will first describe a major karmic event in the early formative years of George W. Bush. When George W. was three years old his Mother gave birth to a daughter named Pauline Robinson, whom the family called Robin. When George W. was seven the Leo/Aries side of his nature was already giving him a reputation as being quite feisty, a bit bossy, and even somewhat of a bully. In relation to his sister Robin, however, his Cancerian qualities became evident. With Robin his behavior was always gentle, caring, patient, and protective. At the age of seven, however, some intense Astrological 'transits' began hitting his birthchart. In February or early March of that year, the elder George and Barbara Bush were told that their daughter Robin had leukemia and would probably die in three weeks. They rushed her to medical specialists in New York and were able to prolong her life for six months until she unfortunately died.

Young George W. knew that Robin was sick, but he was never told that she could die. In his auto-biography George W. says: "I was young enough, and my parents loved me enough, that Robin's death did not traumatize me." In contrast, it has been reported that while feeling betrayed by having the truth kept from him by his parents, George W. cried uncontrollably, slammed the door to his room, and destroyed half of his baseball card collection until his mother stopped him. Later he tried to control his tears, but for years afterwards he would wake up screaming from nightmares. One of George W.'s best friends in child-hood, Randall Roden, remembers sleeping over at the Bush home one night and being awakened by one of George W.'s nightmares, 'It was one of the most realistic experiences I have ever had about death, and I am certain it had a profound effect on him because it had a profound effect on me."[4]

Once again we have another telling dichotomy. Did George W. lie about the more traumatic reactions to his sister's death or did he suppress them from his memory? In any case, Bush now had to endure the pain of such a tragic loss, with parents who hid the depth of their emotional trauma from their children and continued to live in a situation where it wasn't really spoken about. George W.'s Moon in Libra being in tension (square) with his Sun in Cancer accurately reflects the tension between the cheery exterior and hidden interior of the Bush family.

For the Moon in Libra Hilarion says:

This sign is ruled by Venus, the planet of harmony, tranquility, balance, love and beauty. The Moon in this sign at birth denotes an early home environment which was characterized by control of emotional excesses, with at least an outward show of tranquility and harmony. Whether the harmony were really there under the surface can be judged from the degree of affliction to the Moon in this position. A heavily afflicted Libran Moon points to a home life which is superficially smooth and tranquil but with a cauldron of unresolved conflict and turmoil beneath the surface.[5]

In Barbara Bush's memoir she admits that she and George H.W. Bush awakened each night in great pain after the death of Robin, while hating the fact that nobody spoke of Robin, as if she had never existed.[6]

George W.'s brother, Jeb Bush, described this Libran Moon, emotionally controlled atmosphere in their childhood in the following account he gave in an interview with author Bill Minutaglio:

> It goes against how we were...it's just, we are not...it's not natural for us, for, uh, I think I can speak on behalf of all the family, to get into, to be, to turn on this reflective mode and somehow spill our guts,....We were brought up to basically do the exact opposite...and so I think, naturally, it's an uncomfortable thing.[7]

The positive aspect of this Moon to Venus would indicate that a genuine harmony and love did exist in the family. The difficult aspect (square of the Moon to the Sun) would nevertheless show this tendency for things to appear calmer than they were, an aspect of tension especially difficult for George W.'s Sun in Cancer.

It is to the credit of young George W. that he became very concerned about his mother's well being at the time of Robin's death, and it is believed that it was at this time that he tried to uplift the spirits of those around him by becoming the family and later the class clown. His sense of wounding and betrayal, however, still festered. The elder George Bush and Barbara kept trying to have another girl. After another three more boys they finally gave birth to their daughter Dorothy. This was a joyous occasion for all of the other members of the family. It has been noted, however, that George W. was somewhat disconnected and even resentful of Dorothy's arrival:

I'm ashamed to admit it, but I actually hated Doro the first month or two after she was born. No one in the family mentioned Robin's name any more and it seemed to me at the time that everyone was fawning over Doro like she was the second coming of the Almighty. You have to remember I was young back then and confused in my feelings and emotions, but I don't think anyone, including my mother, knew that a little of me died with Robin and seeing this new baby sister only served as a daily reminder for a while of my own personal loss.[8]

George W. was fourteen in the year that Dorothy was born. Carrying the weight of Robin's tragic death in his psyche reflects the propensity of the sign Cancer to become emotionally attached and even possessive of others in relationship. Indeed, part of the karma of a Sun in Cancer person can be met in the following way:

> When an individual expends most of his energy in the nurture of others, there is a tendency to feel that without these others remaining in contact, there will be little substance or meaning left to life. The threat of losing the others...can be expanded into a general feeling of great insecurity on the part of the Cancer individual, for which the only antidote is trust in Providence or God. When several lives are lived in the Cancerian pattern, the feeling of insecurity can become a trait in the soul which requires correction through an incarnational pattern in which events are arranged to increase the feeling of insecurity in the hopes that the individual will ultimately turn to an inner faith in something beyond man.[9]

There is an additional rather heavy element in the karmic experience of George W. Bush. He has the planet Saturn in the Astrological sign Cancer and this Saturn is also in the Twelfth House. If I were with a client now, I would normally say at this point, "And unfortunately, everyone has Saturn somewhere." The location of Saturn in a birthchart indicates where you have to experience karma through a certain heaviness, weight, limitation, or restriction. It is the planet related to the metal lead.

Saturn in Cancer indicates a certain heaviness or restriction in the early childhood. Saturn in the Twelfth House relates to Bush's memory of his most recent past life.

This is what Hilarion says about Saturn in the Twelfth House:

> The placement of Saturn in the twelfth points to a burdened previous life, usually one marked by illness and loneliness. As a result the present personality will bear scars in the subconscious, and these residues may well program him to react to events and people in certain negative ways.[10]

At the time of Robin's death the Saturn in his birthchart was experiencing simultaneous tense transits (squares) from Saturn and Neptune, and a conjunction from Uranus. This heavy Saturnian past life memory was being especially activated at this time.

In another perspective on the Twelfth House, noted Astrologer Liz Greene explains that the Twelfth House represents the inherited family 'daimon,' that is the inherited family unconscious which you then somehow become programmed with. My personal feeling is that the past life memory and the family unconscious are both valid interpretations. With his Twelfth House Saturn, George W. was carrying within him this heavy, difficult, past life memory. It was then arranged for him to incarnate into a family where it was known that there would be a similar heavy Saturnian weight in the family unconscious as well.

Suspended above the family table was a portrait of Robin placed by her father. Her presence was always there, but virtually never spoken about. That the elder George Bush suffered greatly from the loss is revealed in a letter he later wrote to his own mother where he said:

> I sometimes wonder whether it is fair to our boys and to our friends to 'fly-high' that portrait of Robin which I love so much; but here selfishness takes over because every time I sit at our table with just our candlelight, I somehow can't help but glance at this picture you gave us and enjoy a renewed physical sensation of closeness to a loved one.[11]

This letter was apparently written before the birth of Dorothy for in it he pines for a little girl, for some, 'soft blonde hair to offset those crewcuts.' That the elder George Bush would feel these deep feelings but again, not express them, especially with his sons, would, again, relate to the Moon in Libra's tendency to have an appearance of calmness masking more turbulent emotions underneath. That these unexpressed feelings were in fact heavy, deep, and painful would resonate with the Saturn in the Twelfth House, ie. Saturnian heaviness in the family unconscious.

On a more positive note, George W. has his Neptune in the Third House of mind and thinking in positive aspect (sextile) to his Mercury. This aspect would give George W. the capacity to open his mental perspective to the positive aspects of Neptune. These aspects include spirituality and compassion. In addition to being a caring, nurturing Cancer, George W. has, with this Neptune aspect, the ability to express sensitive comments to those around him. These factors also relate to his capacity to open to a religious spirituality. It has been noted that in his childhood his family practiced what has been referred to as a 'Christianity Lite.' It was George W.'s encounter with the Reverend Billy Graham which really helped him to access the potential of this positive Neptune aspect. This opening of himself to God in this Neptunian way positively aspecting his Mercury helped George W. to tone down the arrogance and self-absorption of his Mercury in Leo.

The other factor which would help him greatly in toning down some of the abrasive qualities within his Astrological make-up would be his marriage to Laura. An indication of the destiny for this, by all accounts, happy marriage is Bush's Jupiter In Libra for which Hilarion says, 'In Libra, ruled by Venus, Jupiter always promises an *eventual* happy marriage (or marriage-equivalent).'[12]

This happy marriage and opening to spirituality also helped George W. to finally get a grip on another problem which comes under the influence of the planet Neptune. This problem was George W.'s alcoholism. Neptune, it is to be noted, rules drugs and alcohol. Neptune in difficult aspect will bring lessons relating to confusion, illusion, delusion victimhood and martyrdom. This Neptune in the Third House, the house related to the sign Gemini and to mental thinking, would also resonate with George W.'s tendency to mangle the English language and to be himself victimized for that. Additionally, it would relate to his tendency to use alcohol to buffer himself from the rough edges of life. Some say that George W. was not an alcoholic. His wife Laura said he never drank during the day. Yet, in that time period when George W. was asked when was the last day that he didn't have at least one beer, he couldn't remember. Later, he has stated that his alcohol imbibing days were simply "When I was young and irresponsible." His period of being young and irresponsible, however, lasted until he was 40 years old.

This Neptune is in wide conjunction with his Moon in Libra, the Moon in Libra representing that part of his childhood experience where things appeared as calm on the surface even though they were not underneath. The Neptune is also in tension with (square) his Sun in Cancer. Looking at this complex of factors objectively, with no prior knowledge of the biographical details of the subject, factors involving Sun, Moon, Jupiter and Neptune, I would suspect a very complex relationship between father and son, and perhaps between father and mother, and mother and son.

I have stated earlier in this book that when there is an Astrological complex involving difficult aspects to Neptune it will create what I call a victim/victimizer program. A program such that if you don't want to be a victim you have to be a victimizer. And if you don't want to be a victimizer you have to become a victim. George W.'s experience of this dynamic is a major Astrological theme in his life and a major concern in his performance as president today. It is a theme synchronous with the Neptunian karmic lessons affecting the United States at this time in its history.

Childhood is where these Astrological complexes are usually first created. We then have to deal with the various ways that we unconsciously manifest these complexes in our adult lives. There is one theme evident in relation to the role of the elder George Bush in George

W.'s childhood. That theme is resonant with this difficult Neptune/Sun aspect. Hilarion says Neptune in difficult aspect to the Sun indicates lessons in relation to the individual's experience of the masculine principle. This lesson normally manifests in some difficulty or confusion in the relationship to the father in the childhood. (The Sun is often seen to represent the father in a birthchart.)

There is a recurring theme of a certain Neptunian victimhood and vulnerability in George W.'s childhood in his experience of his father. For starters, throughout the years that George W. was growing up his father was gone a <u>lot</u>. At first, when the young family moved from New Haven, Connecticut to Texas and for a time in California, he was a traveling salesman selling drills to oil rigs, traveling up to 1,000 miles a week. Then he started into the oil business himself, searching for property to buy adjacent to where oil strikes had occurred. For this he would also be away for days at a time. Later George H. W. Bush started his own oil company for which it has been noted that as an independent oilman moving into offshore drilling he traveled even more. Indeed Jeb Bush reflected: "Even when we were growing up in Houston,...Dad wasn't at home at night to play catch. Mom was always the one to hand out the goodies and the discipline. In a sense, it was a matriarchal family."[13]

This had to have been tough on Barbara as the family increased to five children. The Moon being square to the Sun in George W.'s birthchart would resonate with a tension between the parents. Any sense of victimhood experienced by Barbara Bush would, however, remain unexpressed or unapparent because of the Moon in Libra's tendency to manifest a home life which is: 'superficially smooth and tranquil but with a cauldron of unresolved conflict and turmoil beneath the surface.'

In looking back Barbara has begun to express more of how she felt at that time:

This was a period, for me, of long days and short years," she would recall. "Of diapers, running noses, earaches, more Little League games than you could believe possible, tonsils, and those unscheduled races to the hospital emergency room...of feeling that I'd never, ever be able to have fun again; and coping with the feeling that George Bush, in his excitement of starting a small company and traveling...was having a lot of fun."[14]

With George the elder's absence and the fact that George W. was the oldest child, George W. took on more and more the role of surrogate parent to his siblings and surrogate partner to Barbara.

"I look back on those years in West Texas," Barbara recalled, "and I wonder how I would have ever made it without my oldest son. There was never any groaning or moaning on his part [although he did call her the 'Gray Fox' under his breath when she angered him]. I probably put more responsibility on him than I should have, especially for a boy his age," she confessed. "But whom else could I turn to, with his father gone so much in those days?"[15]

George W.'s own relationship to his father was more distant, but psychologically more intense:

"If Mom handled misdemeanors, then it was left to the 'ultimate enforcer' to prosecute felonies. "I would scream and carry on," Barbara said. "The way George scolded was by silence or by saying, 'I'm disappointed in you.' And they would almost faint." Georgie would become particularly upset at the mere suggestion that he might have failed his father. "He could be made to feel," Georgie's brother Marvin said, "that he had committed the worst crime in history."[16]

This particularly acute vulnerability to the reality and presence of his father is a major psychological/karmic dynamic with George W. Bush's experience of himself and life. George W.'s Sun, representing the father in a psychological sense, is in difficult aspect to Neptune, the Moon and Jupiter. Neptune would relate to the sense of victimhood and vulnerability. The Moon would involve the mother. And Jupiter would relate to the elder George Bush having such a major expansive, successful, prominent role in the world around them.

When George W. was born his father was already from a prominent East Coast family, a war hero, a baseball star, and member of Phi Beta Kappa at Yale. When they moved to Midland, Texas, the Bushes were the 'first family' among the other Yankees who had moved to that area. One former friend remembered how everyone called the elder George Bush 'Big George,' and how he "was always the quarterback of the football team, he was immediately in charge and it was so clear that he was the leader of our group, socially and intellectually."[17] Of course later the elder George Bush became an oil millionaire, a congressman, an ambassador to the U.N. and China, head of the CIA, Vice President and then President. A lot to live up to for an eldest son with Leo Ascendant trying to look stronger than he is.

George W. was often the victim of this difficult comparison with the legacy of his father. He followed in his footsteps but, until much later, never as successfully as his father. This path would take him to Andover, the prestigious preparatory school in Massachusetts his father attended. At George W.'s twentieth reunion at Andover he confessed that during his time there he was terrified of failing because of how much Andover meant to his father.[18]

George W. then followed his father's path to Yale, another of his father's alma maters, although his acceptance there has been speculatively linked to family influence. This path also brought him into training as a pilot like his dad. Unlike his father, however, he was spared any real combat. His promotion to lieutenant was on the day of his father's successful election. This path also brought him to the oil business where he never succeeded like his father, and what success he did have was probably, again, due to family connections.

One of George W.'s ways of dealing with his insecurities was through his overindulgence in alcohol. The negative effects of this in relation to his father manifested one night when he drove home inebriated with his brother Neil, crashing into the neighbors trash can. His father was waiting for him, but rather than listen to his father's lecture: "W. burst into the room and confronted his father. "I hear you're looking for me," Junior shouted, shaking his fist...."You want to go mano a mano right here?"[19] As one biographer has stated: "Maybe it was just the alcohol talking. Or maybe it was the nagging frustration of a young man who had come to realize how hard it was to measure up and come to worry about how easy it was to disappoint."[20]

Later George W. claimed that he finally gave up alcohol because it was competing with his affections for his wife and family. These are definitely valid reasons for someone with the Sun in Cancer. Other observers, however, have stated that his motives had more to do with not wanting to disappoint or cause problems for his father, especially as his father started to express ambitions for the presidency.

The experience of the roles of victim and victimizer became more complex in George W.'s relationship to his father when he had to witness the successful, bigger than life George Herbert Walker Bush experiencing his own humiliating defeats and victimizations. He had to witness the abuse and accusations his father had to deal with in his Texan political campaigns. At Yale his father, who supported the war in Vietnam, was condemned by the anti-war students and the liberal faculty. Later George W. took on more and more the role of victimizer of those whom he felt had victimized his father. He was known to be the strong-arm man in his father's 1988 presidential campaign, letting reporters have a 'piece of his mind' if they wrote unflattering or critical articles about his father. Unhappy with one journalist's comments, George W. accosted the reporter and his family during their dinner in a restaurant and yelled: "You no good fucking son of a bitch! I will never fucking forget what you wrote!" What this journalist had written was simply that he thought that Jack Kemp was going to get the Republican nomination for president in 1988. He didn't even mention George Bush in the article. This may seem a minor incident, but I think it is symbolic of a profound psychological dynamic within George W. Bush. It has been conjectured that at least one of George W.'s motivations in running for Governor of Texas was to get back at the incumbent Governor, Ann Richardson, who had stated at the Democratic National Convention nominating Bill Clinton in 1992 that George Herbert Walker Bush was 'born with a silver foot in his mouth.' When

George W. announced to his mother that he was running against Ann Richardson her first reaction was 'Go get her.'

It is also speculated that George W.'s run for the presidency was, at least in part, to get back at Clinton and the Democrats for what they did to his father in 1992. I am sure that George W. has his own sense of service and duty and it has been noted that there were others who put pressure on him to run. One has to ask in the present political climate, however, what really motivates someone to run for president? And, how will those, perhaps, unconscious motives affect their choices and performance as president? Was George W. Bush's attack on Saddam Hussein somehow connected with a festering malice resulting from Saddam's threat to assassinate his father the first President George Bush?

The next section of this chapter will examine how George W. functions as President. The various Astrological factors and formative experiences we have identified can now be observed as they influence the choices and decisions George W. makes. I confess, I did not vote for George W. Bush, and like all humans I am subject to my own biases as I approach political subjects. My skills as an Astrologer, however, have been honed in application to clients whose political affiliation virtually never enters the picture. I have tried to remain as fair and as objective as I can in this analysis of our current president. In this final section of Astrological analysis of George W. Bush I am going to reference the book, 'The Price of Loyalty,' by Ron Suskind. It details the experiences and observations of Bush's former Secretary of the Treasury, Paul O'Neill. He served in prior Republican administrations under Presidents George H.W. Bush, Gerald Ford, and Richard Nixon. O'Neill worked closely with George W. Bush before being dismissed from the cabinet in 2003. His record of public service and Republican credentials make it difficult to dismiss his account as either sour grapes or as liberal ravings.

I would like to begin with O'Neill's description of the 'behind the scenes' White House buildup to the present war in Iraq. Ten days after his Inauguration in 2001, Bush held his first meeting with the National

Security Council. The first topic was the Arab/Israeli conflict. After a short discussion Bush said "I don't see much we can do over there at this point. I think it's time to pull out of that situation." The Secretary of State, Colin Powell, tried to point out that such a hasty exit would likely unleash Ariel Sharon and the Israeli army on the Palestinians. O'Neill noted, 'Bush shrugged. "Maybe that's the best way to get things back in balance."

O'Neill described Powell's reaction as startled.

Bush then turned to Condoleeza Rice and asked what was next on the agenda. She responded, "How Iraq is destabilizing the region, Mr. President." O'Neill says that several observers felt that this interaction with Rice had been scripted. In the ensuing discussion it became clear that there was a pre-orchestrated decision to weaken or terminate Saddam's regime. O'Neill points out that the Council members discussed only the <u>hows</u> of the issue and never any of the <u>whys.</u> This meeting, one must remember, was seven months before September 11, 2001. this unilateral decision to undermine an existing nation clearly violated as O'Neill notes, Bush's campaign promises to be 'humble' in our global involvements and to never engage in 'nation-building.'

A 27 year analyst with the CIA, Ray McGovern, who is part of a group called Veteran Intelligence Professionals for Sanity, states that the President made the decision to go to war first and it was then necessary to find the intelligence to validate the need for that decision. McGovern said that CIA analysts resisted incredible pressure from the Defense Department to state that there was evidence of a link between Saddam Hussein and Osama bin Laden. He went on to say that the administration had deliberately promoted the false story of Iraq allegedly seeking to obtain uranium from Nigeria for nuclear arms production even though that story was a lie based on a forgery.

Confirmationally, in an article entitled, 'The New Pentagon Papers,' published on the internet news and information site, Salon.com, a former Lieutenant Colonel in the Air Force came forth with her observations of what was taking place in the build up to the war in Iraq. She states that after having served in the military for 20 years it terminated with '10 months of duty in a strange new country...'

She confirms what Ray McGovern stated above. She refers to individuals in the Pentagon appointed by the President who manipulated and pressured the interaction between the Pentagon and intelligence agencies. In her own words:

> I witnessed neoconservative agenda bearers within OSP (Office of Special Plans) usurp measured and carefully considered assessments, and through suppression and distortion of intelligence analysis promulgate what were in fact falsehoods to both Congress and the executive office of the president.[21]

That George W. Bush would effectively mislead or even lie to others could easily relate to the effect of Neptune in his chart. This planet creates the propensity for illusion and deception, including self-deception. Compounding this trait is the placement of Jupiter in the Third House in Bush's birthchart. When Jupiter is difficultly aspected, as his is by a square to the Sun, Hilarion states that such an alignment will lead, generally, to a 'dishonest streak.'[22] Moreover, because this is the largest planet, Jupiter, these traits of illusion, deception, and dishonesty can be acted out on a grand scale with far reaching effects. In correspondence with this grand scale are the plethora of books which deal with Bush's tendency to give untrue and deceptive statements.

The Neptunian confusion and delusion of George W. Bush are evident in the following quotes from Suskind's book which I think are quite revealing of how George W. Bush functions as President:

> The problem, O'Neill felt, was that this President's lack of inquisitiveness or pertinent experience....meant he didn't know or really care about the position of the U.S. government. It wasn't just a matter of doing the opposite of whatever Clinton had done, which was a prevalent theme throughout the administration. This President was starting from scratch on most issues and relying on ideologues like Larry Lindsey, Karl Rove, and, he now feared, his old friend Dick [Cheney]. Not an honest broker in sight.[23]

The President was caught in an echo chamber of his own making, cut off from everyone other than a circle around him that's tiny and getting smaller and in concert on everything — a circle that conceals him from public view and keeps him away from the one thing he needs most: honest, disinterested perspectives about what's real and what the hell he might do about it.[24]

Seeing so much of the policy analysis that was being conducted — in so many realms — left O'Neill befuddled about the real intentions that underlay action.

Was it possible, O'Neill wondered, that the country thought it had elected a centrist when in fact it had empowered an ideologue?[25]

The Neptunian illusiveness of the true character of George W. Bush is evident in O'Neill's observations of Bush. O'Neill said he could usually grasp the workings of a prospective employee's mind after a single lengthy interview. Yet after working with Bush for six months, O'Neill felt he still didn't really understand how Bush's mind worked.

Reading 'The Price of Loyalty' book provided a window into what Astrological/Psychological dynamics are at play at the helm of our nation. Essentially, George W. Bush is an insecure man, with a complex relationship with his father, who has used his Leonine and Arian energies of stagecraft, wit and charm (and a good deal of money) to become President of the United States. His own insecurity, coupled with his lack of intellectual engagement and preparation for the task at hand, have made him compensate by surrounding himself with powerful and experienced advisors. These 'handlers' perpetuate the stagecraft upon which Bush relies, both for a semblance of true self-confidence and knowledge, and to also buffer him from the pragmatic realities around him.

George W. Bush's entire life has been based upon appeasing strong powers around him to compensate for his own insecurities and inadequacies. These strong powers around him began with his complex relationship with his father. This legacy continues to reverberate in most of George W.'s later endeavors. These strong powers continue to manifest as the political, religious, and financial forces which enabled George W. to attain his own political successes.

In mentioning the religious powers, one has to look at the power and effect of religion in George W.'s experience of himself. Writers have described the Bush administration as a theocracy, pointing out the heavy reliance upon religious faith and terminology in Bush's political statements. One can surmise that such statements may prove to be no more than political posturing to appease Bush's political base within the Christian Right. Personally, I think that George W.'s faith is deeper and more sincere than that — and more alarming than that.

George W. realized during his conversion experience with the Reverend Billy Graham that he had turned to alcohol instead of God to deal with his problems. Bush's reliance on God to deal with his problems, choices, and decisions can be a similar kind of 'chemical dependence.' It is no accident that Neptune relates to both mystical, spiritual union and to drugs and alcohol. All of these experiences create a dissolving, a surrendering, a freedom from the harsh concrete realities of life. All of these experiences require a strong grounding in concrete reality as it is, for a necessary balance. The positive balance of faith and concrete action will produce someone like Gandhi. A negative imbalance, where religious faith is really a narcissistic ego-inflation or a compensation for insecurity, will produce something along the lines of the Inquisition. It is this kind of danger which scares me when I look at George W. Bush and many of the people behind him.

In the book, *Plan of Attack*, by Bob Woodward, Bush was asked if he had consulted his father before going to war and his reply was: "You know, he's the wrong father to appeal to in terms of strength. There is a higher father that I appeal to."

Now, myself, I also pray to God for clarity and strength in my life. However, for George W. to deflect a question regarding his appreciation and reliance upon his own human father, who had himself served as a president at war with Saddam Hussein, to an assertion of his reliance on God the Father for strength is somehow suspect. This is especially the case when I think of George W's complex relationship with his father and when I look at George W's Astrological aspects. In particular, the aspects involving Neptune, Moon and Jupiter in the Third House of mental thinking and communication, in tension with the Sun (representing father principle). The Jupiter/Neptune component calls to mind something Astrologer Liz Greene said about an aspect involving Jupiter and Neptune. She said that such an aspect will create a situation in which "a sense of absolute moral rightness renders self-questioning superfluous."[26] This statement, in turn, brings to mind some campaign advice given by Bush's right hand man and mentor, Dick Cheney, to associates when he was White House chief of staff in 1976: "Principle is okay up to a certain point, but principle doesn't do any good if you lose."[27]

In relating to George W.'s reliance on God for strength I find my sense of being caught in the crossfire of the current 'culture wars' taking place in this country at this time being stimulated. On the one hand I, along with the Christian Right, am appalled at the torrent of secular obsession with consumerism, sex, and fame, which has created a moral vacuum in much of our affairs. At the same time, I am appalled at the Christian Right's abduction of the moral high ground on these issues, with the attendant obsessive allegiance to a narrow platform of fundamentalist ideology. What is ominous is that people can and often do the most abhorrent things when they think that God is on their side. I believe many liberal, and moderate minded people in this country share this same frustration between these two extremes.

It is George W. Bush's Astrological Karma which has brought him to this position where he must experience the results of his actions. It is the collective karma of the United States of America to have him as our president and to experience the results of his actions.

In the month of the election, November 2004, George W. Bush will have Saturn conjuncting his Twelfth House Saturn by transit. This is the same Saturn which was being aspected at the time of the death of his sister Robin. I am certainly not predicting or hoping that this current transit will result in such a tragic personal loss for George W. It does seem, however, that the time of the election will be a difficult one for him. He will be feeling the heaviness he carries in his own unconscious. In 2005 Saturn will go over his Leo Ascendant and his Mercury in Leo. At that time I predict that he will be deeply humbled, in some manner. His Leonine flair for arrogance and self-absorption will be brought under the heavy leaden hand of Saturn. I personally hope that this will be due to his having lost the 2004 election and then reflecting on the effects of his regime moving into the mists of history. Otherwise, if Bush has been re-elected, I fear what other forces may cause this humbling of our President. On election day, the choice will be ours.

1   *Astrology Plus*, p. 26.
2   Ibid, p. 40
3   *George and Laura: Portrait of an American Marriage*, Christopher Anderson, p. 193.
4   Ibid, p. 38.
5   *Astrology Plus*, p. 18.
6   *Barbara Bush:A Memoir*, p. 49.
7   Interview with Jeb Bush with Bill Minutaglio, found in *First Son: George W. Bush and the Bush Family Dynasty*, Bill Minutaglio, p. 23.
8   *Fortunate Son: George W. Bush and the Making of an American President*, J.H.Hatfield, p. 23.
9   *Astrology Plus*, 6.
10 Ibid, p. 148.
11 *Found in: W: Revenge of the Bush Dynasty*, Elizabeth Mitchell, p. 35.
12 *Astrology Plus*, p. 59.
13   *George and Laura*, p. 48.

14 Ibid, p. 45.

15 *Fortunate Son*, J.H.Hatfield, p. 25.

16 *George and Laura*, p. 45.

17 *First Son*, p. 36.

18 *W: Revenge of the Bush Dynasty*, p. 197.

19 *George and Laura*, p. 109.

20 *Ambling into History*, Frank Bruni, p. 139.

21 *The New Pentagon Papers*, Karen Kwiatkowski, www.salon.com, March 10, 2004.

22 *Astrology Plus*, p. 136.

23 *The Price of Loyalty*, Ron Suskind, p. 126.

24 Ibid. p. 293

25 Ibid. p. 130.

26 *The Astrological Neptune*, Liz Greene, p. 286.

27 Found on p. 178 in *Worse Than Watergate: The Secret Presidency of George W. Bush*, by John W. Dean.

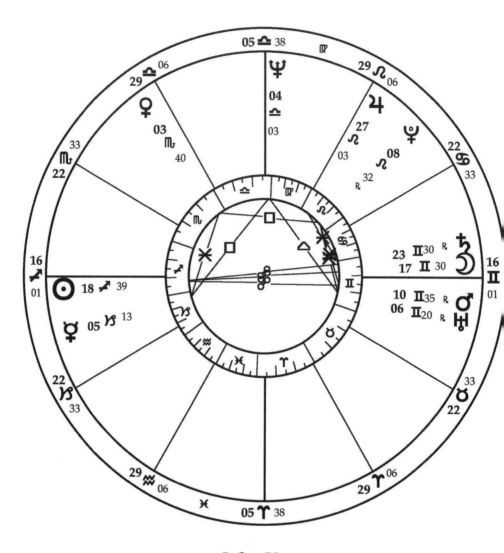

John Kerry
Natal Chart
Saturday, December 11, 1943
8:03:00 AM MWT
Denver, Colorado
Tropical Porphyry True Node

13

THE ASTROLOGICAL KARMA OF
JOHN F. KERRY

John F. Kerry may very well be the next President of the United States. After reading Kerry's book, *A Call to Service*, I believe that his desire to serve this nation is sincere. I would endorse, for the most part, the coherent vision he has mapped out for America to fulfill her promise. And yet, who is this man really?

My examination of John Kerry's Astrological karma has both disclosed his genuine ethical leadership capabilities and unveiled some of his difficult karmic challenges. Studying a person's Astrological birthchart enables us to 'read between the lines' of their life history. I find it fascinating to see specific factors in a birthchart and then discover the ways in which those factors have manifested in that person's life. When I first examined John Kerry's birthchart, for example, I immediately noted that his political career could create stress in his marriage/relationship experience and lead to divorce. I later learned that Kerry had been married previously. His first wife Julia said that the stresses of being a politician's wife were the underlying cause for their divorce.

I do feel positive in relation to the fact that Kerry is a Sagittarius, born on December 11 when the Sun was in the sign Sagittarius. The positive aspect of a Sagittarian Sun is described by Hilarion:

> The Sagittarian is one who, in a past experience, lived a life of honor, integrity and uprightness and who showed to others these qualities in so consistent a fashion that the others were positively helped in their spiritual progress by the experience. The result of the life of honor is a tap into the highest possible spiritual source of such urges, so that they are always available to the soul and to the personality, filters permitting.[1]

'Filters permitting' refers to the matrix of factors and influences which may obscure the connection to the energies of one's Sun sign. With Kerry's Sun situated in Sagittarius, however, I have no doubt that his moral integrity is genuine and sincere. In addition to his Sun in Sagittarius Kerry also has his Ascendant, representing his self-image, in the sign Sagittarius. In Astrological parlance we would say Kerry is a double Sagittarius.

We previously examined the qualities of a Sagittarian Ascendant represented in the self-image of the United States. These characteristics emphasize a love of travel and adventure blended with a positive enthusiastic 'can-do' spirit. Kerry's self-image echoes these favorable Sagittarian features which explains his lifelong attraction to what we now call 'extreme sports.' He rides a Harley Davidson motorcycle, plays hockey and flies small airplanes. Kerry's cousin remarked that when young John rode his bicycle he was always racing, never just calmly pedaling along. At age sixteen, after persuading his reluctant father, Kerry rode a ferry from Norway to England where he bicycled around the countryside.

The fact that Kerry appears so unemotional and controlled much of the time has a lot to do with his Libran Midheaven of which Hilarion says:

> Libra at the M.C. [Midheaven] will indicate one who habitual-ly projects an image of refinement, calm and emotional control. These traits are often not really present in the make-up of the individual. The intent of placing Libra on the Midheaven is to prompt the person to increase his control over the emotional nature, ...[2]

So Kerry is not as calm as he looks.

There is one facet of people with Sagittarian Ascendant that often makes me apprehensive. Hilarion cautioned that having a Sagittarian Ascendant: 'will tend to make the individual see himself as upright, honest and morally strong, whether true or not.'[3] This potential self-deception is interwoven with childhood, relationship, and other issues that will challenge Kerry with difficult karmic lessons. Such lessons are part of everyone's life, so let us now look at the particular forces at play in John Kerry's life.

Kerry has the Sun in the First House of self-image, which Hilarion describes as follows:

> Since the first house represents the ego-view or self-picture (as we have already explained), then it follows that the Sun in the first suggests that the self-image will strongly pre-occupy the mind, that the thoughts, attitudes and habits of the "native" (the person whose chart it is) will be colored by a tendency to dwell on the self and to see others and the environment as secondary in importance. "Self-absorbed" will often be an appropriate adjective. Naturally, a person can learn, through persevering effort, to overcome this self-orientation of the mind (just as all negative or unbalanced traits can be corrected).[4]

With Kerry's Sun being in Sagittarius I have no doubt of the essential genuineness of his moral integrity. This inclination to be self-absorbed coupled with the karmic lesson resulting from having the Sun in Sagittarius would tend to rub people the wrong way at times. The specific lesson for a person with Sun in Sagittarius is:

> The task of the Sagittarian is to utilize the urges and to demonstrate uprightness again in this life without allowing the excessive emphasis on honesty and candor to hurt others. It can happen that the Sagittarian is so determined not to hide anything that he fails to consider his thoughts before he gives utterance to them. Not pausing to think of what effect one's words might have on another can lead to embarrassment, awkwardness, and even pain — even though the inflicting of discomfort or pain on another was the farthest thing from the Sagittarian's mind. The major lesson then is not to blurt out thoughts without thinking first what effect they might have on another.[5]

I often observe that Sagittarians are subject to what I call, 'foot in mouth disease.' They fail to sense the feelings of others when overwhelmed with their impulsive honesty. When Kerry neglected to check out whether a conversation was private before passionately denouncing the Bush re-election campaign as: 'The most crooked....you know, the most lying group I've ever....'; a live microphone captured his candor. Kerry's earnest sincerity and the tendency to be self-absorbed drew attention to Kerry's ambition while he attended St. Paul's Preparatory School in New England. While there he didn't hide his ambitions. He started the John Winant Society debate club and openly expressed his hope of becoming a politician. It has been noted that 'such raw ambition rubbed some schoolmates the wrong way.'[6]

Our Astrological analysis so far has shown that Kerry's ambition and frank honesty express his Sun in the the First House influence. His sincere motivation to serve his country with 'honor, integrity, and uprightness' radiates the essence of a Sagittarian soul. But are these attributes sufficient to compel Kerry to seek the Presidency in the current abrasive American political arena? Hilarion provides another clue from the Sun in the First House to help us to understand Kerry's drive:

> Another direct effect of the Sun in the first is to add a note of power to the personalty. There is always a distinct aura of will and strength present in the picture that the individual projects to the world, whether or not those traits are components of the higher self.....Usually such an overlay effect is deliberately added to the personality in order to compensate for a conviction of inferiority arising from episodes in previous lives. Thus it will often be observed that one with the Sun in the first is adept at projecting a facade of strength, will and control over the environment, while inwardly there lurks a desperate fear that others will one day discover the incompetence or the unworthiness or the self-embarrassment which constantly echoes, like a mocking laugh, up from the depths of subconscious recollection.[7]

Thus Kerry with his First House Sun and Bush with his Leo Ascendant have both been provided with powerful self images to compensate for their inner perception of insecurity or unworthiness arising from their previous lives. It seems that gaining the Presidency is one way to placate those persistent doubts and fears.

Our examination of the Sun in Sagittarius and Sun in the First House demonstrate the strengths and challenges Kerry has been endowed with in his traits of ambition, impulsive honesty, moral integrity, and the capacity to appear strong and in control. Kerry's Sun in the First House, however, was placed in his birthchart opposite to some severe tempering influences. Kerry's Sun is opposite to Mars, opposite to the Moon, and opposite to Saturn. We Astrologers euphemistically label these aspects, or alignments, as 'great opportunities for growth.' These are major Astrological configurations which have affected Kerry in many different ways at many different times in his life.

The Moon's placement reflects the Astrological influences apparent in Kerry's childhood. The Moon itself is in Gemini, of which Hilarion says:

> This sign is ruled by Mercury, the planet of the rational mind. The Moon in this segment will always show that the early home influence, as perceived by the child, was one of mental stimulation and an emphasis on achievements of the thinking or rational faculty.....the positive side of the Gemini nature as manifested in the home environment, ...will usually cause the individual to seek a home in his mature years which is enlivened by study, mental stimulation, much chatter and conversation, and so forth. This desire for mental stimulation in the home may also manifest as a more or less regular changing of address, especially since this is also likely to have been a characteristic of his own early home experience.[8]

Kerry's family moved frequently during his childhood due to his father's diplomatic career in the U.S. Foreign Service. As a child Kerry bounced between New England and Europe, attending a variety of schools. He reminisced that as a child, "I was always moving on and saying goodbye."[9] The mental stimulation at home and parental emphasis on mental achievements has been mentioned in many observations of Kerry's childhood. The Moon is also conjunct to Saturn which injected a particularly heavy, brooding, even suppressive influence into Kerry's childhood. The Saturn in his birthchart is in Gemini, which Hilarion describes as:

> In Gemini, Saturn denotes a tendency for the mind to be too serious and weighed down.[10]

This Saturn reflects much of John Kerry's experience of his father, Richard Kerry. When Richard Kerry was only six years old his own father committed suicide. Richard Kerry has been described as having a 'brooding intellect.' When he was upset about something he would stare out at the ocean for hours, 'engulfed in a deep contemplative mood no one wanted to disturb.'[11] Kerry has described his father as "painfully remote and shut off."[12] The challenge for John Kerry has been to navigate around the deep whirlpools of mental brooding while paddling ahead with the intellectual skills developed as a child and polished in his political career.

Saturn's alignment opposite to the Sun provides Kerry with lessons involving conflict with authority figures. Richard Kerry disciplined his children, especially his sons, so that, 'diligence, duty, and loyalty were instilled in them, with tenderness usually coming last.'[13] I believe it is no wonder that the young Sagittarian John Kerry often got on his bike and raced away to escape that heavy, brooding Saturnian authority. As he himself has later stated: "My bike was sort of my great escape from parents and rules and all those things."[14]

Saturn's opposition to the Sun also exacerbates the struggle of Kerry's Sagittarian enthusiasm resisting suppression by a Saturnian energy of duty and restriction. Kerry remembers how his father chafed at the limitations imposed by the bureaucracy of the diplomatic corps. His father had idealistically joined the U.S. Foreign Service believing he could positively impact the world. Instead he became increasingly frustrated by endless restrictions, eventually departing his career 'disillusioned and disappointed.'

Although these tensions emerged in John Kerry's childhood they remain part of the karmic lessons he must heal and integrate in his adult life. There are various ways in which the dichotomy between an exuberant Sagittarian energy and a restrictive, weighed down

Saturnian energy have manifested and continue to do so in John Kerry's life. Before discussing some of those manifestations, it is important that we first explore the influence of Kerry's Moon in the Seventh House. This is the arena of relationships, which Hilarion outlines as follows:

> Here we have a lunar placement which is extremely revealing of certain traits of the native. Specifically, this position points to one who in past lives has eschewed the company of others to such an extent that in the present experience, there is a strong tendency toward isolation and a desire to be "left alone."
>
> Yet this trait is not one that will help weld the human family together, as the Aquarian Age requires. Therefore it is mandatory that any with the Moon in the seventh — particularly if strongly afflicted — must be thrown again and again into the company of their brothers. Only in this way can they learn to enjoy human contact.[15]

To sum up, we have a Sagittarian First House Sun brimming with enthusiasm, honesty, and righteousness, who is adept at projecting a facade of strength, will, and control over his personal environment. These qualities, however, are in opposition to, and compete with the Lunar preference for privacy and rational deliberation as well as the mental seriousness of Saturn and its burden of authority. The dichotomy between these two potent dynamics in John Kerry's psyche has frequently manifested in conflicting behaviors.

When Kerry was patrolling off the coast of Vietnam on board the Naval ship Gridley, far from firsthand combat, he learned that his dear friend Richard Pershing had been killed in battle. In a letter to his parents he stated his desire to make a better world and to "end once and for all this willingness to expend ourselves in this stupid, endless self-destruction."[16] In contrast, Kerry said in other statements that he wanted to avenge the death of Pershing and wanted to transfer to where he could 'feel the war.' Kerry was consciously aware of this conflict within himself, noting that he wanted the Paris Peace talks to succeed and that he also wanted to see action.

Later when he was finally given an assignment to a combat position a 'piqued and unenthusiastic Kerry packed his duffel bag....As loath as he was to go, however, something in him thrilled just a little at the prospect of heading into the unknown. By the time he had to leave Cam Ranh, an almost perverse excitement crept into his demeanor. It was in that curiously conflicted mood that Kerry took the wheel of PCF-44.'[17] Kerry commanded a 55 foot long swift boat which patrolled the narrow waterways of the vast Mekong River Delta. Naval leaders planned Operation Sealords to intentionally draw enemy fire with the loud U.S. boats and then have them respond with devastating fire-power. American casualties soared with 75% of the sailors killed or wounded, while many innocent Vietnamese civilians were slaughtered in the murderous rake of gunfire. Kerry's opposition to the wasteful war intensified as he began to fear that careerism in the Navy's upper ranks had something to do with it — after all, the more headlines and medals a commander's men earned, the greater his chance of making admiral.

John Kerry was wounded three times under fire yet his willingness to engage in combat has evoked contradictory reports. One former crewman said "He absolutely did not want to engage the enemy when I was with him. He wouldn't go in there and search."[18] On another occasion, however, Kerry went beyond his orders, beaching his boat and pursuing an enemy combatant on foot until he killed him. This courageous albeit reckless type of action forced a superior officer to question whether Kerry should 'be given a medal or court-mar-tialed.'[19]

The paradox of Kerry's reactions to combat frames a reluctance to engage in battle, exhibiting the traits of isolation of Kerry's Moon and the insecurity behind the bravado of his First House Sun, in confronta-tion with the Sagittarian traits of righteous enthusiasm and First House self-absorbed ambition and ability to mask those fears through a projection of strength and courage. Kerry's karmic challenge is to acknowledge these competing dynamics and harness their energies to serve his country with honor and integrity. When he returned to the

U.S. after combat service, Kerry harshly criticized the continuing American military involvement in Vietnam. His fervent Sagittarian passion and serious Saturnian mental energy were successfully integrated when he spoke to the Senate Armed Services Committee in April, 1971. After an eloquent, determined and inspired delivery, Kerry boldly asked the Senators, "How do you ask a man to be the last man to die in Vietnam? How do you ask a man to be the last man to die for a mistake?" It is that kind of conviction, integrity and serious application which makes me believe that John Kerry could be a capable President of the United States.

In reviewing Kerry's life what surprised me the most was his enlistment in the Navy after strongly opposing the Vietnam War for several years. His father criticized the U.S. military intervention from its inception, even while serving as a U.S. diplomat. John Kerry delivered his first public speech as a junior at Yale. He summarized the history of Vietnam and then called for a complete U.S. withdrawal declaring that 'the South Vietnamese government had fallen into disarray, anti-Americanism pervaded Southeast Asia, the Johnson administration's policies were failing, and the domino theory was a myth.'[20] Kerry concluded by stating that it was vitally important for the U.S. to gain military victory or negotiate a peace in order to save face. As a senior at Yale Kerry was chosen to be the speaker for his graduating class. He spoke at length on the failure of American foreign policy and the futility of the war in Vietnam.

The insightful analysis of U.S. and Vietnamese history displayed in these speeches once again underscores the Sagittarian honesty and integrity and Saturnian, rational seriousness. Yet a short time later Kerry reversed course and enlisted. As Kerry's combat experience intensified so did his inner psychic battle. Even though he felt more opposed to the war than ever, he also felt even more 'compelled by patriotism to fight it.'

Kerry also began to feel a growing sense that he had been deceived. He remarked to a fellow officer in Vietnam, "Nobody has been able to tell me why we have to do what we're doing here. Nobody can really explain in terms that make sense why it is [that] the United States has to be the one to lose its men and spend its money for a supposed threat, which few people can define. Besides, I don't see how what we're doing is helping the Vietnamese anyway."[21]

I believe the element of self deception may have tipped the balance between the conflicting Astrological tensions and impelled Kerry to enlist. The source of this deception is Kerry's capacity to delude himself about his own beliefs and actions. What is troubling is the lack of awareness of this powerful current of self deception that is helping shape the course of his life. The tendency to see himself as upright and morally strong, whether true or not, flows from his Sagittarian Ascendant. The U.S. birthchart echoes this delusional tendency which contributed to our misguided military intervention in Vietnam.

When more than two hundred Madrid train commuters were killed in the recent 2004 terrorist bomb attacks, the newly elected Spanish President began to follow through on his campaign pledge to withdraw troops from Iraq unless there was greater United Nations involvement. Kerry quickly urged the Spanish President to reconsider and not withdraw troops at such a critical stage in the occupation of Iraq. I spent three months in Spain in 2003 without meeting a single person who supported Spain's military presence in Iraq. The Spanish and other European nations willingly contributed military and financial support to the 2001 invasion of Afghanistan to destroy Al-Qaida terrorism and overthrow the Taliban who sheltered them. By contrast, the Spanish and most U.N. nations balked at supporting the U.S. invasion of Iraq because Saddam Hussein's government had not sheltered or supported Al-Qaida. Eight out of ten Spaniards were opposed to their nation's involvement in Iraq prior to the Madrid bombings.

For John Kerry to press the Spanish to maintain their military commitment in Iraq disregards their mourning and insults a proud nation's honor. Kerry's insistence illustrates the deceptive lure of moral certainty, whether true or not, cast by the Sagittarian Ascendant. Such moral conviction, without sensitivity and intellectual integrity, is just arrogance with a fancy name. This tendency towards self-justified deception helped launch American accusations that a Spanish withdrawal would appease the terrorists. Such claims demonstrate our national insensitivity and/or ignorance of the Spanish having endured the terrorist attacks of the Basque separatists for the past thirty years.

The self-deceptive tendencies may also be derived from Kerry having Mercury square to Neptune in his birthchart. Such an afflicting aspect between these two planets would subject him to confusion, illusion, and deception. The Mercury is in Capricorn which in itself is another factor engendering a serious frame of mind. This Mercury is also in Kerry's First House, the arena of self-image. At the 1971 Vietnam Veterans Against the War rally in Washington, D.C. many veterans threw their ribbons and/or medals at the Capitol building. Kerry kept his medals while throwing his ribbons and somebody else's medals. At the time, however, he claimed the had thrown his own medals. A minor incident perhaps, but it raises questions about his motivations. The Sagittarian Ascendant and Neptunian potentials for deception can be not only a deception of others, but a self-deception as well.

Kerry's statement about the Spanish troop withdrawal has been criticized as political pandering. Others contend that it demonstrates that Kerry would lead the U.S. in cooperatively working with other nations rather than going it alone. By either interpretation, Kerry was also clearly motivated by his Sun in the First House ambition, which helped propel him into politics as a school boy.

Kerry's individual karmic challenges and psychological dichotomies do parallel several of those in the U.S. birthchart as discussed previously. What gives me hope is that John Kerry could be the next figure to conjoin his individual karma with our collective karma. As Kerry becomes more aware of his own spiritual lessons to be learned, his progress could serve as a catalyst for the U.S. to raise its consciousness. Instead of stumbling into Neptunian self-deception and illusion we could gracefully surrender to Neptune's powers of healing and compassion and manifest true honor and integrity.

Kerry has his Neptune conjunct to his Midheaven. This union would produce a quality of compassion in the way he which he would seek to present himself to the world. His Neptune is in positive aspect to his Mars in Gemini, putting a powerful, sharp intellect in service to that compassion. Kerry's genuine concern for the suffering of Vietnamese civilians was served by his intellectual and political efforts to end U.S. involvement in the war. Uranus is conjunct to the Mars and trine, or positively aspecting, the Neptune thus producing a quality of freedom and liberation from old limiting views and energies as part of this powerful mental energy in service to compassion. Kerry rose above the tenacious perception of Vietnam era division between liberals/doves battling conservatives/hawks to reach across to fellow Senator John McCain, a former Vietnam P.O.W., and together draw up legislation to heal the P.O.W./M.I.A. anguish for American families and restore normal relations with Vietnam. The Mars/Uranus conjunction is also placed in Kerry's Sixth House of work, service, and activity in the world. These beneficial qualities of compassion, intellectual energy, and independent thinking percolate through Kerry's daily activities.

As I write this in May, 2004, I can see the next year will provide John Kerry with promising opportunities in politics, personal growth, and marriage. In November, 2004 Kerry has positive Jupiter transits occurring which indicate that he may well be feeling quite pleased on election day. I make this election prediction after also looking at the more depressive transits hitting Bush at that same time. In 2004 Pluto is on Kerry's first House Sun in Sagittarius which should be leading him into some deep introspective honesty and soul searching. The deep transformative potential of Pluto may also ignite an integration of Kerry's identity with the potential to be a powerful means of transformation in the lives of others.

In 2005 Pluto will move into opposition with Kerry's Saturn in the Seventh House bringing about potential change and conflict into his marriage. Hilarion discusses how the Moon in the Seventh House influences marital relationships:

Usually, a person with a seventh house Moon will find that periods of his life are marked by many ups and downs in terms of his love-partner or marriage. Often, two permanent marriage-like associations will be experienced.[22]

And for Saturn in the Seventh House:

The placement of Saturn in the seventh sector points to the karmic necessity for enduring a traumatic break-up of a marriage or marriage-like bond.

However, unless Saturn receives only adverse aspects from other planets, the native will likely not be denied married fulfillment permanently. Provided he seeks earnestly the key to understanding why the marriage foundered, and strives to make the necessary changes in himself, it is likely that, at least eventually, a suitable match can be made which will be permanent.[23]

On an optimistic note, Kerry's Saturn does have a very positive sextiling aspect to Jupiter. I therefore feel hopeful for his current marriage to Teresa Heinz Kerry, provided that Kerry has learned from the mistakes made in his prior marriage. It seems that ex-wife Julia was blaming Kerry's all-consuming political career for the traumatic breakup of their marriage. In her book, A Change of Heart, she said: "Politics became my husband's life,....After 14 years as a political wife I associated politics only with anger, fear and loneliness."[24]

So what will happen when Pluto opposes Kerry's Saturn in the Seventh House of Relationship? In some ways the outspoken Teresa seems more Sagittarian than Kerry. In comparison Kerry seems more like the subdued Saturn influence. As the media spotlight intensifies, will Teresa respond publicly to criticism of herself or of her husband? Perhaps Pluto's impact to their marriage will be confined to the Kerry bedroom as part of their own growth and evolution.

If John Kerry does lose the 2004 election it could well be due to energies derived from yet another factor related to Kerry's First House Sun.

That factor is:

> The main karmic significance of this placement is the necessity to pass through many testing periods in terms of the ego or self. In numerous cases a breaking down of the old pattern is necessary, and this may come about through a nervous crisis, through a severe depression or through manipulation by others — for example in any of a number of "cult" groups presently on the earth which practice confrontation as a technique to secure the obedience of members. This karma arises from a past life in which similar pressures were applied against others, always with a retarding influence on the soul-growth of those affected.[25]

As far as I know Kerry has not been involved in any "cult groups." And for you conspiracy buffs I don't think the Skull and Bones Society at Yale classifies. Kerry has, however, had to frequently deal with the efforts of others to manipulate and control him in order to secure his obedience.

Soon after returning from Vietnam in 1970, Kerry joined the rising tide of public opposition to the Vietnam War. He became a spokesman for the Vietnam Veterans Against the War to protest the Nixon administration's continued U.S. military involvement there. As Kerry's leadership and public visibility increased, Nixon and his cohorts retaliated. Kerry was added to Nixon's infamous 'enemies list' which secretly targeted individuals and organizations perceived by Nixon as enemies. His administration then illegally used government agencies such as the FBI and IRS to discredit and threaten these opponents into submission. FBI records have since surfaced documenting the agency's close surveillance of Kerry's activities during this period.

A Nixon operative, Charles Colson, who served as legal counsel to the President before being convicted of helping to cover up the Watergate affair sent a letter in 1993 to Kerry apologizing for: "having tried to undermine him [Kerry] when he was head of the Vietnam Veterans Against the War. I think there were some stories that Nixon and I were trying to find as ways to discredit him, and I am sorry for past feelings resulting from anything I have done."[26]

These controlling and manipulative forces hit Kerry hard and often during his first campaign for Congressman from Massachusetts. The local newspaper ran a major smear campaign which resorted to character assassination of Kerry. Professional hecklers routinely jeered him during campaign speeches. It was common knowledge that his telephone was tapped, making a clicking sound every few moments. Leaflets claiming Kerry was a drug addict appeared. These tactics culminated when three days before the election, the candidate in third place, running as an independent, suddenly dropped out of a very tight race. Rumors surfaced that this candidate made a deal to throw his votes to Kerry's main competitor in exchange for his campaign debts being quietly paid off. When Kerry lost the election it was later revealed that President Nixon had waited up on election eve to confirm Kerry's defeat before going to bed satisfied.

These efforts to control and manipulate Kerry provided him with a 'testing period in terms of the ego or self.' They may have been karmic payback for Kerry's own efforts to pressure others in a prior life, as suggested by Hilarion's comments on the First House Sun. These tests appear to have reminded Kerry of the need for safeguards against such coercion and manipulation. "The experience of having been spied on for the act of engaging in peaceful patriotic protest makes you respect the civil liberties and the Constitution even more."[27]   These trying experiences may have also contributed to Kerry's willingness to investigate associations such as international crime syndicates and those involved in th Iran-Contra affair in the late 1980's.

With Pluto currently conjuncting Kerry's First House Sun, I am sure that he can feel the deep underground investigation by the Bush forces into every past statement, vote, or other activity of his which they could manipulatively use against him. Just like President Nixon attempted to discredit Kerry, President Bush is attempting to do the same thirty years later. Vice President Cheney has orchestrated attacks by himself and designated Republican Senators to distort Kerry's combat service records. On the surface this may appear to merely be a Republican maneuver to deflect questions regarding Bush's own military service records. Given the Bush parallel to Nixonian duplicity and the current conjunction of Pluto, however, I believe Kerry may once again be experiencing his karmic challenge relating to manipulative and controlling forces.

Kerry demonstrated an awareness of these forces while campaigning in the 2004 Florida primary. He was asked how Democrats can be assured that the Republican forces in Florida would not once again undermine the voting process. (For a detailed account of the hidden machinations in the 2000 Florida election results I recommend Greg Palast's book *The Best Democracy Money Can Buy*). Kerry responded that the new electronic voting machines recently purchased by Florida Governor Jeb Bush's administration needed to also have a back-up paper trail of how votes were cast in case those machines malfunction.

The point here is that it is no accident that John Kerry has the karmic necessity to confront these controlling/manipulative forces. Fortunately he has the sincerity and enthusiastic conviction to fight hard against these forces. All we can do is to each make our own best efforts, and then let God do the rest.

1   *Astrology Plus*, p. 10.
2   Ibid, p. 33.
3   Ibid. p. 27.
4   Ibid, pp. 91-92.
5   Ibid. pp. 10 - 11.
6   *Tour of Duty*, Douglas Brinkley, p. 33.
7   *Astrology Plus*. p. 92.
8   Ibid. p. 15.
9   www.wikipedia.com, John Kerry
10 *Astrology Plus*. p. 67.
11 *Tour of Duty*, p. 29.
12 *John F. Kerry: The Complete Biography by the Boston Globe Reporters Who Know Him Best*, Michael Kranish, Brian C. Mooney, Nina J. Easton, P. 22.
13 *Tour of Duty*, p. 19.

14 *John F. Kerry: The Complete Biography*, P. 23.

15 *Astrology Plus*, p. 112.

16 www. wikipedia.com

17 *Tour of Duty*, p. 153.

18 www.boston.com, The Boston Globe online archives, Michael Dranish, March 11, 2004, quoting Steven Gardner.

19 www.wikipedia.com, John Forbes Kerry.

20 *Tour of Duty*, p. 55.

21 Ibid, p. 182.

22 *Astrology Plus*, p. 113.

23 Ibid. p. 145.

24 Found in: *John F. Kerry:The Complete Biography*, P. 185.

25 *Astrology Plus*. p. 92.

26 www.wikipedia.com, John Forbes Kerry.

27 www.wikipedia.com, John Forbes Kerry.

14

SUMMARIZING GEORGE W. BUSH
VS.
JOHN F. KERRY

Comparing George W. Bush and John F. Kerry one can see that both of these men are mere mortals. They each have their own virtues and their vices. One can surmise that if Bush had been born into a Democratic household his Cancerian caring, nurturing qualities would have born out under a Democratic banner. By the same token if Kerry had been born into a Republican household his dynamic Sagittarian righteousness may have fought for Republican causes.

Both of these Presidential candidates have character traits that trouble me. With Bush it is his propensity for deception, the tendency to use arrogance to cover up his insecurities, and the unconscious alignment with a victim/victimizer program. With Kerry it is his rather extreme dichotomies and the tendency to use bravado to mask his own insecurities. As far as their political policies I happen to be in greater agreement with Kerry's platform. In the final analysis, I would say that the self-righteousness and dichotomies of Kerry scare me less than the false arrogance and dishonesty of Bush.

As I said earlier, the intense Plutonian transits hitting the U.S. chart right now will continue into 2006. Whoever is President in the next four years will be linking their personal Astrological karma to the collective Astrological karma of this nation. It is a momentous choice we face at this time. The election of one of these candidates may well lead us deeper into a Holy War. It would have America travel through major conflict and destruction to reach a rebirth into a New Age. The choice of the other candidate offers more opportunity for a peaceful transition into this new era. I pray that we choose wisely.

15

CONSPIRACY THEORIES AND
THE PROBLEM OF EVIL

As one who has taken upon himself the task of trying to make sense of what is happening in the U.S.A., I am constantly confronted with the myriad of conspiracy theories which are now in circulation. I am aware that a certain amount of conspiracy may be percolating beneath the surface appearance of things. As previously stated, I personally do not believe that Lee Harvey Oswald acted alone in the assassination of President John F. Kennedy. I do not believe, however, that President Bush and his cohorts orchestrated the events of September 11 or consciously colluded with those who did. I do believe that Bush and his cohorts have shamelessly exploited the fear generated by 9/11 to implement their own agenda.

I am amazed by the number of people I meet who earnestly believe that a conspiracy of all powerful, dark evil forces are manipulating events for their own ends. To these people I often ask the question: "If Bush and the CIA actually orchestrated 9/11 then why haven't they found weapons of mass destruction in Iraq by now? Why haven't they just placed them in some remote site of discovery?" Now if weapons of mass destruction are discovered in Iraq a week before the 2004 election when Bush is trailing in the polls, I may have to rethink everything I am about to say.

The American people are particularly susceptible to swallowing whole these conspiracies of nefarious masterminds. Our belief systems are inclined towards illusion and confusion when influenced by our Ninth House Neptune in tension with the Mars in Gemini in our birthchart. Accentuating this gullibility is the obliging Sagittarian Ascendant tendency to see ourselves as honest, upright, and morally strong, whether true or not. In my work here and abroad I have observed that Americans tend to believe in things that people in other countries would never believe in.

I personally feel the promoters of many of these conspiracy theories are themselves being influenced by what the Ascended Master Hilarion calls The Dark Forces. In his book: *Dark Robes, Dark Brothers*, Hilarion explains that there are dark forces and that they are part of God's plan. God created everything including the dark and the light. The truth is, without darkness there is no concept of or possible experience of light. It is the opposing darkness which tests us in our growth towards the light.

Hilarion describes how the dark forces attack those individuals who are already on the path of spiritual development. The dark forces work through certain teachers, gurus, or channeled entities who possess a lot of truth and wisdom. Their truth and wisdom, however, is carefully interwoven, consciously or unconsciously, with things that are not true. When these untruths, concealed within a larger body of information, are accepted by an unsuspecting seeker they thwart his/her spiritual progress. I feel that this sinister design has ensnared many of the conspiracy theorists, for the most part unconsciously. These individuals have enough genuine truth and wisdom to make the distorted message appear believable.

I suspect that one intended effect of the dark forces scheme is to marginalize people away from the mainstream. If a person really believes many of these theories, for example that the Illuminati/One World Government or the Reptilian Aliens are in control of everything, then why would they bother to vote in the next election?

Hilarion goes on to say that the Spiritual Hierarchy, cannot divulge who is good and who is bad because this situation serves a purpose. The purpose is for us to develop our own powers of discrimination.

Hilarion says elsewhere that if anything doesn't seem right to you, then you should reject it, because either it means it isn't right or it is simply information which you at this time are not capable of benefitting from. In either regard you are totally justified in rejecting it.

Hilarion does confirm that the Anti-Christ energy exists on this planet today. He explains that just as the Christ is really an energy and not limited to the incarnation of one historical person, so too the Anti-Christ is an energy and it dwells within elements of the Political, Business, and Military aspects of society.

I have a hard time, nonetheless, with people who have more compassion for Osama Bin Laden than for George Bush. To me there is too great a temptation to want things to be black and white. This temptation is to always blame events on a bad guy, whether it be George Bush, Bin Laden, or the Reptilian Aliens, instead of accepting that we are all just frightened little girls and boys doing the best we can.

Personally, I am grateful for my faith in the Ascended Masters and the Spiritual Hierarchy in service of God/Goddess/All that is as being the true ultimate power behind the events and evolution of life on this planet. I am grateful for my faith that behind all of the darkness and pain and suffering there is a higher plan of karmic evolution and the ultimate spiritual liberation of the human family.

.

16

THE PURPOSE OF EXISTENCE

In respect of the previous discussion and in response to questions sparked by the discussion, 'The Experiment of Oceania,' I have been inspired to share some of my general thoughts on the purpose of existence. My perspective has evolved over many years and consists of a synthesis of knowledge from many sources. One of the more satisfying sources of insight into the purpose of existence is the knowledge contained in the books on Kabballah by Zev Ben Shimon Halevi. I personally feel that Halevi is the best public Kabbalistic teacher in the world today. There may be other private teachers whom I am unaware of.

Kabbalah, for those unfamiliar, is a body of knowledge and practice generally seen as the inner esoteric teachings within Judaism. Halevi has pointed out that the Kabbalistic schools which flourished in the South of France and the North of Spain in the 14th century were never limited to only Jews. Any sincere seeker of deeper spiritual knowledge and experience was allowed to enter those schools.

The Kabbalistic view of the purpose of existence, in my understanding, is essentially for God to become known to Itself. In Kabbalah they speak of God the Transcendent and God the Immanent. God the Transcendent transcends any existing thing, any idea, any concept. It is beyond anything that can be known. When God was God the Transcendent, however, God was God, but God had no way of knowing God was God. By a complex process, God allowed a portion of itself to enter into a state of limitation, to enter into existence. This is God the Immanent, God in manifestation.

The reason that it is necessary for our souls to experience an involution (spirit coming down into form) into a physical body is because it is in this state of concrete physical limitation, the densest level of existence, that we experience the illusion of separation from the One.

It is in this illusion of separation, however, that we are able to experience autonomous, independent free will. Our purpose then is to explore what we do and don't want to do with that independent free will. In that process we must experience the expression of our free will within the confines of the established laws of the universe. These laws include the law of cause and effect which operates at not only the physical level. The operation of cause and effect on other non-physical levels amounts to what esotericists call the law of karma or, as Jesus said: "As ye sow, so shall ye reap."

In experiencing the results of our actions in the expression of our independent free will, we hopefully progress to where all we want to do is to serve the will of God. This leads to a reuniting with our creator, where the knower and the known become one. In this regard we are truly the children of God. When we reunite with the One, however, we do not lose our independent free will. We, in effect, become co-creators with our creator.

This was the true message of Jesus. 'The Aquarian Gospel of Jesus the Christ,' a book channeled from Angelic Messengers tells the true story of the life of Jesus, including the so-called 'lost years' of his life. After the Resurrection Jesus is quoted as having said: "My human will was wholly given to bring my will to tune with the Deific will.....I lived to show the possibilities of man. What I have done all men can do, what I am all men shall be."[1] To me, this was the true message of Christ, not the politically controlling, judgment and guilt producing belief systems spawned by churches bearing his name.

I do agree with the Fundamentalist Christians belief that one must surrender to Christ to enter a state of heaven. Unfortunately the Fundamentalist concept of surrender implies that one need only make a personal testimonial to Jesus. I believe one must fully surrender to the Christ spirit, the Love of God made manifest, an experience which is at the heart of the inner teachings of all the great religions.

1 *The Aquarian Gospel of Jesus the Christ*, by Levi.

17

2012 AND THE END OF THE MAYAN CALENDAR

Within the alternative culture there is a growing attunement, and anticipation related to the year 2012. This phenomenon has been fueled by authors who have researched and expounded upon the significance of the Mayan Calendar. The Mayan civilization flourished in Central America prior to the arrival of European explorers. The Mayans had developed the most sophisticated calendar in human history. They applied their advanced knowledge of astronomy and mathematics to formulate a precise calendrical time system featuring various cycles of time, each set within larger cycles of time. According to the Mayan calendar the current cycle of time began in 3113 BC and will end on December 21, 2012. This cycle is the last period in an even larger cycle of 26,000 years.

Profound transformation of the Earth is predicted to occur by various authors. When this cycle ends on December 21, 2012 some say that our planet is then going to enter the photon belt, thereby eliciting major changes in consciousness. Others say that on the Winter's Solstice of December 21, 2012, the Sun will be in direct alignment with the 'Galactic Center,' or midpoint of our Milky Way Galaxy, which will generate major changes in consciousness.

At my lectures people often ask if I see any Astrological corollary relevant to the purported transformation predicted for 2012. The Master Hilarion has said nothing about the significance of 2012 and he is the source I trust most on such cosmic matters. I did look into my Astrological ephemeris to see how the planets would be relating to each other in and around the year 2012. I was startled to see a powerful Astrological alignment appearing in that time period. This particular aspect most recently occurred during the Great Depression and the rise of fascism in the 1930's.

This approaching alignment merits serious consideration as it has the potential to serve as part of an Astrological 'trigger,' to stimulate transformations of a much greater cosmic scope. The aspect I am referring to is Uranus moving into a square to Pluto. In the 1960's these two planets made a conjunction. When two planets conjunct it represents the planting of a seed which then goes through a cycle of growth. We can observe this cycle in the example of the phases of the Moon. First there is the planting of the seed in the New Moon in which the conjunction of the Sun and Moon begin the cycle. This is followed by the First Quarter in which the Moon is square to the Sun. Then the Full Moon with the Moon opposite to the Sun. Then the Last Quarter in which the Moon is again square to the Sun, and then the end of that cycle and the beginning of another in the next New Moon conjunction.

Pluto and Uranus were most recently square to each other in the 1930's, a concluding phase of that previous cycle. In the 1960's a 'New Moon' or new cycle of growth was initiated when Uranus and Pluto again conjuncted with each other. Pluto represents a slowly building yet intense transformation, bringing things up from the subconscious or the 'underworld.' Uranus signals a sudden, surprise transformation producing immediate freedom and liberation. In their 1960's conjunction, Uranus spurred a sudden and revolutionary transformation in society, transformation which had been slowly building in the Plutonian underworld for many years.

Those of us who experienced the 'Sixties' can say that it was clearly a time of major transformation on many different levels. That time period was also a time of 'seeding,' of planting the energies for this new cycle. Since that time period the evolution of consciousness has proceeded more slowly, maybe not in terms of technology, but in terms of consciousness. If I were to bring myself back to the year 1970 and imagine where I thought the world would be in terms of consciousness in the year 2004, I must say, it would be a lot further along than where we are now.

The upcoming Pluto/Uranus square, however, gives me renewed hope for our planet. I realize now that the time period of the late 60's and early 70's, was the time for the seeding of a new consciousness into the planet. This seed has been growing largely underground, not surfacing onto the cover of Time Magazine or to the conscious attention of many who had received this seed in the 1960's.

When the planets Uranus and Pluto form their square to each other in 2012 it will be the first major test as to how well we have, collectively and individually, lived up to the message and intention of that seed planted four decades ago during the previous 'New Moon' conjunction of these two planets. There were many different messages promoted at that time. I personally think the Beatles gave us the most simple and succinct expression of that era in the words of one song: "Love is all there is."

I predict that as we approach the year 2012 there will be, once again, a period of major upheaval and transformation and a new awakening of consciousness. I am quite curious to see what the experience and expression of this transformation will be for those who were born between 1962 and 1976 during the period of effect of the Uranus/Pluto conjunction. I have already observed that many in this generation realize that they missed something. I have heard many say: "I was born at the wrong time. I wish I had been able to experience the sixties." These regrets emanate from being born with the Astrological imprint of that era, an imprint which engraved the energies and consciousness of that time period into their being.

As far as what Astrological karma will be affecting the United States in particular on and around the year 2012, I was startled to see the intense effect of this conjunction upon the U.S. Birthchart at that time.

Pluto will be continuing to be move through the First House of self-image of the U.S. This will continue to force either deep introspection and transformation of our self-image or the expression of 'blind and irrational ego forces.' Pluto will no longer be in close aspect to the Mars/Neptune square. That particular tension will have passed. During the years leading up to and following 2012 Pluto will, however, be making oppositions to the U.S. Venus, Jupiter, and Sun.

These three planets, Venus, Jupiter and Sun are all positioned in the U.S. Seventh House of partnerships and relationships. Therefore intense karmic exams in relation to our relationships with others will continue to be an on-going theme in the years ahead.

These three planets Venus, Jupiter, and Sun are also all in the sign Cancer, a sign of caring, nurturing and devotion, or of emotional possessiveness. What will all of this mean? I can imagine various scenarios depending largely upon what kind of collective consciousness we are manifesting at that time.

Venus and Jupiter in the Seventh House generally engender positive, harmonious relationships with others. These Pluto transits could force us, once and for all, to look deeply into all of the dysfunctional attitudes and behaviors which keep us from relating to our brother/sister nations in the world in the most positive, harmonious ways.

Pluto opposing our Sun in Cancer in particular will force us to really own that we are truly a Cancer nation. As I said earlier, the best symbol of the Cancerian, caring, mothering quality of the U.S. is the Statue of Liberty. The Statue of Liberty bears the poem offering to care for the 'poor and huddled masses' of the world. During these upcoming transits we could rise to the glory of conscious awareness and manifestation of all that the Statue of Liberty represents. This could be when the U.S. manifests Hilarion's prediction that: 'In the new age that will dawn for mankind, America will lead the world as a great and burning beacon of truth, of justice, of peace and of purity.'

I continue to have faith that that will be the ultimate destiny and manifestation of consciousness in the United States. I still fear what growth lessons we will have to endure before coming to this awakening. The positive predictions for the United States in Hilarion's book, *The Nations*, were published in 1984, based on conditions at that time. I sometimes fear that the United States, through its own free-will actions, especially through many rather negative actions, has altered that destiny, placing a darker shadow upon our future.

I have given the more positive vision for the experience of the U.S. in 2012. If we are manifesting more of the fear and greed based elements of our being at that time I envision these approaching transits in 2012 with a more somber foreboding.

The Sun in Cancer has the negative tendency to be overly possessive of those whom it cares for and nurtures. Additionally, our Sun, being in the Seventh House, bears this karmic lesson in relationships:

> From the lesson point of view, this sun position calls the native to acquire a sense of proportion and balance in his attitudes toward "the other",......On the one hand, there is too strong an emphasis on the importance of the partner in one's life, while on the other hand there is a tendency to try to manipulate and control that other so that the native's pre-conceived ideas about how a love partnership should function will come true. Alas, the usual result of such manipulation is the very opposite of the native's desires: it is to drive a wedge of resentment between him and the partner. If he is perceptive, he will realize at last that the partner is a fully independent individual and should be cherished and honored and loved for what he is, rather than being coerced into conforming with the native's fantasies of what should be.[1]

If the United States continues to remain oblivious to the reality of its effect and relationship with the rest of the world, if it continues to coerce others into conforming with our fantasies of what should be out of our own fear and greed then this Pluto opposition to our Sun will serve as a serious wake-up call.

A telling statistic: Of all of the developed nations of the world the United States gives the lowest, per capita, amount of foreign aid in the world. In a national survey it was discovered that the majority of Americans feel that we give too much foreign aid. When asked how much foreign aid would be appropriate the amount stated is usually two to six times more than what we actually give.

If this kind of self-absorbed, greed and manipulation is what we are collectively manifesting as we approach 2012 I feel that this future time period is either when the entire world will have had enough of us and will stand against us, or it will be when the results and effects of our actions and manipulations have resulted in such negative manifestations that we are forced to face the truth of ourselves.

There is an additional part of our Astrological exams in 2012 I have not yet mentioned. In 2012 transiting Uranus will have entered the Fourth House of the U.S. birthchart. The Fourth House is related to the sign Cancer. It is the house of home, family, childhood, sanctuary, roots, of your psychological 'base.' Uranus, the planet of sudden, surprise, transformation, liberation and freedom will tend to manifest sudden changes in your experience of home and family and of sanctuary when positioned in the Fourth House.

I spoke earlier about the global effect of Uranus moving in to square to Pluto. I said that square would be the 'First Quarter' test of the seed that was planted during the New Moon Pluto/Uranus conjunction in the 1960's. The United States will be personally experiencing this Pluto/Uranus square in the following way: Pluto will be in the U.S. First House of self-image. Pluto will also be in opposition to the Venus, Jupiter and Sun in the U.S. Seventh House of relationships. Uranus, in the sky, will move into the U.S. Fourth House of home and sanctuary and form a square to transiting Pluto in the sky. Uranus will also be moving into squares to the U.S. planets Venus, Jupiter and Sun in its Seventh House of relationships.

What will be the effect of this Uranus tension in our Fourth House of home and sanctuary? Again, I can imagine various scenarios. This could result in the eruption of a new Uranian, 1960's-like movement of liberation and transformation manifesting within our own national borders. A liberation from old inappropriate ways of being and consciousness. This could force a sudden transformation of the Pluto/7th House relationship lessons then taking place. This change would be to a more honest regard for ourselves and compassion for others.

The less positive vision of these transits upon the U.S. would be to envision the intense effects of the Pluto/7th House relationship lessons manifesting suddenly, violently, within our own home, within our own borders, within our own sanctuary. These sudden, perhaps violent, Uranian events would then force us to deal with the effects of our self-image in relation to others, and thus lead to a more honest regard for ourselves and compassion for others. As to which scenario is likely to appear, as I said earlier, the choice is ours.

I interviewed a Mayan Priest and his wife from the Yucatan Peninsula in Mexico asking what they thought would be the significance of December 21, 2012. They replied: "All we can say is that at that time everyone on the planet will have the opportunity to choose. They will have the opportunity to choose Love or Fear."

---

1 *Astrology Plus*, pp. 98-99.

18

AFTERWORD

In the middle of the Canadian film *The Barbarian Invasions*, which won the Oscar for best foreign film at the 2004 Academy Awards, the audience observes a television broadcast of the attack on the World Trade Center. A commentary on the significance of the tragedy follows in which the September 11 attacks are compared to the first barbarian incursions into the core of the mighty Roman Empire. These audacious assaults by uncivilized tribes against the invincible Roman heartland appeared foolhardy and insane. Yet these raging heathens were united in their hatred of the most dominant economic and military power to overrule the world.

Such a comparison may well be considered hyperbole, or perceived as a thought-provoking perspective. I am sure the Romans never imagined that those early raids would lead to the collapse of their empire. Similarly the American public seems unworried despite the dire predictions of those seeking to capitalize on the situation. Two months after the September 11 violence, however, the *International Herald Tribune* newspaper polled 275 opinion leaders throughout the world seeking their reaction to the horrific events. More than two thirds of the foreign responses agreed that it was 'good that Americans now know what it's like to be vulnerable.' More than half supported the conviction that many or a majority of individuals believed that 'American policies or actions in the world were a major cause of the September 11 attacks.'[1]

In preparation for writing this Afterword to this book I read several recent books on American and world history, politics, and philosophy to gauge the flow of world events. A profoundly adept insight into the world situation is provided in: *Jihad vs. McWorld: Terrorism's Challenge to Democracy*, by Benjamin R. Barber. The author expands the definition of Jihad beyond the traditional Islamic meaning of 'holy war' to include a 'disintegral tribalism and reactionary fundamentalism.' Similarly his definition for McWorld includes the 'forces of integrative modernization and aggressive economic and cultural globalization.' Even though these forces flow from a variety of nations, Barber contends they follow a distinctly American template.

Economic observer Amy Chua goes further, perceiving a heavy-handed U.S. promotion of crude capitalism:

> ....terms such as "market economy" and "market system" refer to a broad spectrum of economic systems based primarily on private property and competition, with government regulation and redistribution ranging from substantial (as in the United states) to extensive (as in the Scandinavian countries). Yet for the past 20 years the United States has been promoting throughout the non-Western world raw, laissez-faire capitalism — a form of markets that the West abandoned long ago. The pro-capitalism measures being implemented today outside the West include privatization, the elimination of state subsidies and controls, and free-trade and foreign investment initiatives. As a practical matter they rarely, if ever, include any substantial redistribution measures.[2]

Barber claims that the true victim in the clash between Jihad and McWorld is democracy itself. He portrays this conflict quite poignantly in the following paragraphs:

> ... the spiritual poverty of markets — may bear a portion of the blame for the excesses of the holy war against the modern; and [that] Jihad as a form of negation reveals Jihad as a form of affirmation. Jihad tends the soul that McWorld abjures and strives for the moral well-being that McWorld, busy with the consumer choices it mistakes for freedom, disdains. Jihad thus goes to war with McWorld and, because each worries the other will obstruct and ultimately thwart the realization of its ends, the war between them becomes a holy war....Reasoned communication between the two is problematic when for the partisans of Jihad both reason and communication appear as seductive instrumentalities of the devil, while for the partisans of

McWorld both are seductive instrumentalities of consumerism....

Should would-be democrats take their chances then with
McWorld, with which they have shared the road to modernity
but that has shown so little interest in them? Or try to reach an
accommodation with Jihad, whose high moral purpose serves
democracy's seriousness yet leaves but precious little space for
its liberties? As it turns out, neither Jihad nor McWorld — and
certainly not the quarrel between them — allows democracy
much room.[3]

The conflict which Barber eloquently describes is a global phenomena. And yet, any U.S. citizen who has spent considerable time abroad
can recognize that an American fueled economic ideology and power
dominates the world as thoroughly as do our military forces. This
power and ideology stresses free market capitalism with little or no
government regulation. Under the influence of this ideology the world
economy has increased on average 2.5% over the last ten years. In that
same period the number of impoverished people has increased by 100
million. The top 1% earn as much income as the bottom 57% of the
world's population. And the disparity is increasing.[4]

The three most powerful forces propelling economic globalization
are the International Monetary Fund, the World Bank, and the World
Trade Organization. The leaders of these organizations are appointed
rather than democratically elected and thus not accountable to the citizens of member nations. These organizations conduct most of their
business behind closed doors and are dominated by the U.S. and routinely recite its corporate mantra of 'free markets.' The dogmatic
attempts to convert everything in our lives into commodities for sale
in these artificially rigged 'free markets' has produced absurd scenarios worthy of a Mark Twain or Tom Robbins.

For example the 'free' market zealots in these organizations and
multi-national corporations consider even the water people drink to be
a resource that should be exploited through private ownership. An
American corporation persuaded the Bolivian government to allow

them to privatize that nation's water supplies. Water is often scarce there due to the high and dry mountainous terrain. The price of water soared by 50%, threatening the economic survival and health of many subsistence farmers and their families. As the profits rose ever higher, the insatiable corporation then pressured the Bolivian government to prohibit any person from collecting rainwater because it would be 'unfair competition.'

The dominance of U.S. economic power and its hidden manipulation of organizations and governments is reflected in our birthchart most strongly by Pluto in the Second House of money and finances. Pluto's placement here amplifies the abundant resources for material success and the powerful karmic lessons summoned by its obsessive pursuit. In addition, the U.S. Pluto also resides in the sign Capricorn, an Astrological sign related to material ambition. Earlier in Chapter Four I discussed the force and the below the surface maneuverings of this Astrological factor. At the time of the writing of that chapter the scandal at Enron was current news. We Americans have since learned that that scandal was just the tip of an iceberg of American corporate greed and malfeasance.

What has become ever more clear to me now are the global repercussions of American Plutonian power and obsessiveness. The Astrological array of Plutonian financial obsession coupled with a Sagittarian Ascendant self-righteousness and a Seventh House of Martial aggressiveness in relationships has produced an economic imperialism so pervasive that 50% of the world beyond our borders feel that 'American policies or actions in the world were a major cause of the September 11 attacks.'

In *Jihad vs. McWorld* Barber does acknowledge the benefits of capitalism as an effective and efficient means of production. Capitalism's primary motive and focus is on its bottom line profit motive, however, which does not engender social justice, sensitivity to the needs of the environment, or a deeper spiritual quest. Many of my friends in Europe suggest that the world needs 'Socialism with a brain' combined with 'Capitalism with a heart.' They feel that governments practicing socialism without a brain and capitalism without a heart have caused a great deal of social and economic misery. I think, however, that these systems are becoming irrelevant as we head deeper into the emerging paradigm of the Aquarian age. Aquarius is a sign of equality and brother/sisterhood. It is also a sign of group consciousness. I see both communism and the rise of multi-national corporations as early, primitive responses to the incoming energies of the Aquarian Age. Hilarion predicted that the reason Communism would fail is because men will never recognize that they are truly brothers until they can acknowledge they have a common father. Indeed the only times that Communism seemed to create a sense of comradeship among its citizens was when they were led by a strong father figure such as Lenin or Mao Tse Tung. These human 'fathers,' however, inevitably fail in the larger task of unification of people at the transpersonal or soul level.

Corporations embody a group consciousness that extends beyond individual identities and national borders. Although their pursuit of profit is often detrimental to spiritual and social values, corporations and their international marketing are inexorably advancing a global consciousness and awareness. Corporations present us with the paradox of horrification at their devouring McWorld appetite for ever larger markets and programmed consumers balanced against a deep appreciation for their encouragement of the emerging global consciousness. As awareness of how humanity is deeply interconnected spreads, the corporate model of group consciousness demonstrates how people can cooperate and operate independent of national borders and self-interest.

Another excellent book I have been reading since writing the first edition of this book is: *The American Soul: Rediscovering the Wisdom of the Founders,* by Jacob Needleman. The author evokes a resonance with the American Soul. He states that America is the only nation in the world which is based on philosophical ideals. America is not based on a 'tribal, ethnic or racial identity.'[5]

Needleman delves into the minds and hearts of Benjamin Franklin, George Washington, Thomas Jefferson, and Abraham Lincoln, to discover an honoring and appreciation for what America was based on and could yet become. He presents commentary and prose from Walt Whitman, especially the 'Democratic Vistas' which Needleman says 'May justly be considered the most powerful manifesto ever written about the meaning of American democracy.'[6]

> I say that our New World democracy, however great a success in uplifting the masses out of their sloughs, in materialistic development, products, and in a certain highly deceptive superficial popular intellectuality, is, so far, an almost complete failure in its social aspects, and in really grand religious, moral, literary, and esthetic results. In vain do we march with unprecedented strides to empire so colossal, outvying the antique, beyond Alexander's, beyond the proudest sway of Rome....It is as if we were somehow being endow'd with a vast and more and more thoroughly appointed body, and then left with little or no soul.[7]

I wonder how Whitman would regard our present state of affairs. The materialistic malaise portrayed here by Whitman more than a century ago is interpreted by Needleman as a disease of the mind which is starved for ideas and which can only lead to despair. Needleman chastises the failure of America to live up to its potential mission. He points out that America is not superior to the rest of the world. He calls America a 'conduit for the forces of modernity,' whose duty is to provide a safe haven for these transformative energies.

Needleman goes on to warn:

> The world will see that it needs this entire America, America with its soul. It does not need and will absorb, resist, imitate and dissolve an empty America. A metaphysically empty America cannot endure, it will not survive; it may keep its name and armies for a while, it may keep its Constitution and its laws and forms of government, it may keep its symbolic heroes, it may remain a place where people wish to survive physically and economically; but without the inner resonance of its ideals and values....without its American soul, America is sure to go nowhere, and, if so, where will humanity go?[8]

Needleman further points out the necessity to note the difference between what America *is* and what America *means*. He states that we are naive:

> ...when our feeling of hope is directed toward the outer America that we perceive with the senses, rather than the America we grasp with the mind and the heart. because this other America seems powerless or elusive does not mean it is not real. Because America betrays its ideals is no reason to reject the ideals themselves. We do not live in correspondence with the great life hidden within us; but that is no reason to deny that this hidden life exists and calls to us.[9]

The karmic destiny of America to wield its material power in synthesis with the 'great life hidden within us' is something which the approaching years will address. In 2008 Pluto will move into the sign Capricorn and will remain there until around 2025. In 2023 the U.S. will have its first 'Pluto return,' the return of Pluto to its natal position in our birthchart. Hilarion says that someone who is born with their Sun in the sign Capricorn is someone who has in previous lives accomplished a lot and helped others in a material way. This past life experience gives the Capricorn a lot of ambition, a desire to make something of themselves in the eyes of the world, and a lot of self-reliance. That self-reliance, however, is where the Capricorn tends to put their faith.

Hilarion states:

> ....because the help for others was limited to the material plane, a blindness is introduced into the make-up of the Capricornian personality which makes it more difficult than usual to perceive the reality and value of spiritual concepts and the higher wisdom.[10]

I predict that while Pluto, that great 'bringer of change,' is moving through Capricorn the ability to base one's life upon exclusively materialistic goals will become increasingly difficult. The United States with its natal Pluto in Capricorn could well be a symbolic focus or primary actor on the world stage playing out this transformational process.

This material life transformation process may well be related to the fact that a growing consensus of petroleum geologists predict that global oil production will peak somewhere in the period between 2006 and 2015.[11] When this peak in oil production occurs oil will become an increasingly scarce resource demanding increasingly higher prices. In the face of this reality the entire global economic system must come to a rude awakening. The choices we make at that time are critical to the fate of the planet.

Hilarion has predicted that a final global conflict could occur as a result of the nations of the world fighting over ownership of the Middle-East oil deposits. This is one possible response to the diminishing availability of the oil/life blood of the current world economy. Another response would be to reassess our current way of life. We could awaken to the relative insanity of lifestyles based upon the obsessive consumption of non-renewable resources in pursuit of material luxury. As our eyes cleared we could clearly see this materialistic, consumptive craving, which I compare to methamphetamine addiction. Like a drug high, it feels so good that you want to go faster and faster, while at the same time it is totally destroying all of your internal organs.

With the United States consuming 25% of the world's resources with only 5% of the world's population we are the largest symbol of this modern materialistic obsession. One commentator stated that the first Iraqi Gulf War was undertaken in defense of the 'American way of driving.'

In the Tarot reading I did for the U.S. on the evening of September 12, 2001, described in Chapter 9, the card for the overall outcome of the cycle of events then being examined was The Devil. Interestingly, The Devil card itself corresponds to the Astrological sign Capricorn. Capricorn is an earth sign related to the principle of mountains, which can represent a great obstruction. They make it difficult to travel from one area to another. On mountains it is difficult to raise food and physically sustain oneself. And yet, it is the reality of mountains which have always served as an inspiration for humankind to aspire towards and commune with that which transcends the world which can only be known with the five physical senses. This obstruction/transcendence is resonant with the symbolic experience of the entire physical plane and its illusion of separation. This physical identification is a great blockage and limitation of consciousness, and yet, overcoming that blockage and lifting that limitation is a tremendous liberation and spiritually empowering experience. Indeed, after referring to the difficulty for a Capricorn personality to perceive the reality of and value of spiritual concepts, Hilarion goes on to state:

> Though difficult, it is not impossible, and the Capricornian who succeeds in making of his life a dedication to a higher reality achieves far more and conquers a much greater obstacle than most other souls have to contend with.[12]

The significance of the Devil card is an initiation where you must face your own Devil, that which blocks or limits you from being who you really are and can be, seeing clearly the illusions about yourself which you have believed, but which are not really true. I hold to the hope and the faith that the United States will face its own Devil. Imagine our nation seeing clearly the illusions about ourselves and our nation which we have believed, but which we finally realize are not really true. As America regains her vision with the death of material illusion and rebirth of freedom, her success can inspire a global death and rebirth into a new age of universal love and brotherhood. The labor pains we have to endure in that process is related to our own surrender or resistance to that process.

I pray for us all.

Easter Sunday, 2004.

1   Found in *Granta: The Magazine of New Writing*, Granta 77 -
     Spring 2002, Pg. 12.
2   Wilson Quarterly, Autumn 2002, article: *A World on the Edge*,
     by Amy Chua, p. 73.
3   *Jihad vs. McWorld: Terrorism's Challenge to Democracy*,
     Benjamin R. Barber, p. 215.
4   Statistics found in *War Talk*, Arundhati Roy, p. 70.
5   *The American Soul: Rediscovering the Wisdom of the Founders*,
     Jacob Needleman, p. 39.
6   Ibid., p. 360.
7   *Democratic Vistas*, Walt Whitman, found in *The American Soul*,
     p. 320.
8   *The American Soul*, p. 343.
9   Ibid. p. 332.
10 *Astrology Plus*, p. 11.
11 Statistics originally published in *The Party's Over: Oil, War and
     the Fate of Industrial Societies*, by Richard Heinberg, found in
     Smoking Gun: The CIA's Interest in Peak Oil, Richard Heinberg,
     www.museletter.com.
12 *Astrology Plus*, p. 11.

19

FINAL AFTERNOTE

Earlier in this book I stated the significance of the 'Progressed Sun.' This is an Astrological technique where you move the position of the Sun one degree for every year of your life. It is one of the best indicators of movement and change in consciousness and identity through a birthchart. In an article entitled *'The Dawning of a New America*, by Astrologer Robert Blaschke,[1] he points out that the Progressed Sun of the United States will enter the sign Pisces on November 1, 2004 — one day before the U.S. presidential election. This progression into Pisces will continue for 30 years thereafter.

The Sun in Pisces placement in a birthchart, according to Hilarion, indicates a soul who in some previous lifetime went through an experience of emotional pain that was so great that it led them to take their own life. This previous life experience leaves the Pisces individual in this life with an echoing memory of sadness and sorrow. This memory of sadness also enables the Pisces individual to tune in to the sadness in everyone else. Hilarion goes on to say that this increased sensitivity also gives the Pisces the capacity to make of their heart a well of compassion for the needs and sufferings of others. This compassion for others is in fact the best way for them to overcome and transform their own sadness. The lesson for the Pisces individual is to avoid trying to escape the harshness of life through Neptunian temptations (Neptune rules Pisces) such as overindulgence in drugs or alcohol.

On election day this nation will be newly born into the sign Pisces. This will be a new entry into a new emotional sensitivity. If Bush is re-elected those who support him, who may even believe he is God's choice for this time in history, will be relieved and comforted in their emotional, devotional aspirations. Those who oppose Bush's re-election may feel that George W. Bush's first term was prelude. Now we will have to be really vulnerable to the negative side of Pisces, which is rather synonymous with the negative side of Neptune i.e. illusion, confusion, delusion, victimhood and martyrdom.

If John Kerry is elected those who oppose his bid for the presidency will be feeling those negative Neptunian/Piscean qualities. For those who support Kerry, there will be relief and hope that we really can enter into a quality of emotional compassion and sensitivity extending to all who suffer within or outside of our borders. This new compassion and sensitivity may take some time to manifest, but I predict that it will do so eventually, even if Bush is re-elected. From November of 2004 until 2017 our Progressed Sun will be making positive, harmonious, 'trining' aspects with the placements in the US. birthchart of Venus, Jupiter, and in 2017 with the U.S. Sun itself. This deeper unconscious movement in identity will be occurring at the same time that the Pluto/Uranus square mentioned in the chapter about 2012 will be tensely aspecting these same planets. I predict that this new Piscean sensitivity, in positive aspect to these caring, nurturing, Cancerian planets, will lead to a new consciousness and emotional maturity which will reflect Hilarion's prediction:

> At last, in an agony of the soul, America will again stand forth with her love, to rescue and nurture the peoples of the world whose nations have collapsed and disintegrated in the terrors that man has brought upon himself. By that act she will again and for all time be purified. In the new age that will dawn for mankind, America will lead the world as a great and burning beacon of truth, of justice, of peace and of purity.[2]

As I said the last time I typed in those words, all I can say is: Amen.

---

1   *The Dawning of a New America*, Robert Blaschke, The Mountain Astrologer magazine, April/May 2004, p.9.
2   *Nations*, Hilarion, p. 23.

Appendix

THE ASTROLOGICAL SYSTEM

In the following pages I will provide a brief introduction to the symbols and language of Astrology. The material contained there should assist those unfamiliar with Astrology to appreciate the discussions ahead. I would like to note here that one of the dangers encountered in Astrology is a tendency to 'not be able to see the forest because of all the trees.' An Astrological chart holds a vast amount of information. This is why, in private readings, I always tape record the session. The tape can be used afterwards to continue to digest the information. In this present instance you of course can re-read this book.

Astrology is a symbolic system. A system whose mode of operation is such that the moment of one's birth is purposely arranged to occur at a time when the heavens symbolically reflect the pattern of lessons, characteristics and experiences which have been chosen for that individual to work on and grow through in that lifetime, based on their previous life karma. The following discussion will explain the functioning structure of this symbolic system.

The Planets And Signs

The word planet, coming from the Greek language, means 'wanderer.' The stars, relative to our view from the earth, remain fixed in their positions in relation to each other. In contrast, the planets appear to move or 'wander,' against the backdrop of the patterns of stars in the sky.

As they travel, the planets and the Sun and Moon move through a limited band of the sky. The circle which serves as the medial axis of this band is known as the 'ecliptic.' The ribbon of star patterns which serve as the backdrop for this movement of planets, extending approximately 8 degrees above and below the ecliptic, is called the Zodiac.

The word zodiac is derived from two Greek words meaning 'circle' and 'animals.' The zodiac is divided into twelve sections, corresponding to twelve constellations of stars. These are the twelve so-called 'signs' of the zodiac.

The planets move through the different constellations or signs of the zodiac at quite different speeds. The Sun moves through the entire circle in a year's time, the Moon in approximately 28 days, and Pluto in 247 years.

The following are the symbols and a brief description by Hilarion of the significance of each of the planets:

☉ - The Sun - Denotes characteristics which are a predominant feature of the soul or higher self which has projected the personality.

☽ - The Moon - The Moon is related to the ideas of nurturing and domesticity, and in particular often tells of some trait or traits which the native developed as a result of his early home experience.

☿ - Mercury - Connected with the mind, the ability to think rationally, communication with others. Indicates the mental abilities, talents, habits.

♀ - Venus - The planet of love, art, beauty, affection and togetherness. Shows the nature and direction of the love impulses.

♂ - Mars - Represents the energy with which the physical body carries out its various functions; muscular, mental, emotional and procreative. A gift from the will/power/creativity part of the divine triangle.

♃ - Jupiter - Represents the idea of bigness, increase, growth, expansion, assimilation. It relates to higher education, travel, religion and higher philosophical thought.

♄ - Saturn - The most significant indicator in the sky of what is essential for the individual to understand about himself or herself. Saturn's position indicates much in terms of voluntary or imposed blockages and restrictions of a karmic nature.

♅ - Uranus - Governs all that is eruptive, unexpected, unusual, or occult. Indicates the ability to throw off restrictions and strike out on a new path.

♆ - Neptune - Rules the Sea. Associated with altered states of consciousness, mysticism, and the astral plane. Can indicate confusion or delusion or an aspect of spirituality.

♇ - Pluto - The planet Pluto is the great bringer of change. Where this planet is located in the birth chart always designates an area or department of life in which the soul has agreed to undergo pressures promoting a deep-seated alteration in its attitudes, habits or understanding. If the personality resists these pressures, then much stress and difficulty will be felt. Pluto is like the irresistible force, sweeping all before it. The only beneficial approach to this planet's energies is to move in the direction it indicates. To do otherwise is to invite disaster.

The following are the symbols and names of the twelve zodiacal signs:

♈ - Aries   ♎ - Libra

♉ - Taurus   ♏ - Scorpio

♊ - Gemini   ♐ - Sagittarius

♋ - Cancer   ♑ - Capricorn

♌ - Leo   ♒ - Aquarius

♍ - Virgo   ♓ - Pisces

The Houses

The twelve 'houses' of the Astrological system represent particular departments of life where the individual planets play out their roles, as influenced by the zodiacal sign they bear. In the Western Astrological system the position of the Sun on the first day of spring is always attributed to the first degree of the zodiacal sign Aries.[1]

The twelve houses symbolically resonate with and follow the same order as the twelve zodiacal signs. The houses are not determined by the movement of the planets, but instead by the Earth's complete rotation in 24 hours. In this manner all of the planets are seen to move through all of the twelve houses in 24 hours.

For example, twelve to thirty-three years of people will be born with Pluto located in the same zodiacal sign. Whereas people born on the same day and in the same place, but minutes or at the most 3 hours apart, will have Pluto in a different house. The house placement therefore will often indicate a much more individual and specific influence than the zodiacal sign placement of the planet. This is especially the case when considering the slow moving 'outer' planets, such as Uranus, Neptune and Pluto.

The arrangement of the houses is structured such that a line drawn to the eastern horizon when you are born is referred to as the 'Ascendant,' and is the cusp or 'beginning' of the first house. The first house is related to the sign Aries and to the spring equinox. The sign on the eastern horizon at birth is referred to as the Ascendant or 'Rising' sign.

A line drawn to the western horizon is called the 'Descendant, and serves as the cusp of the seventh house, related to the sign Libra and the Autumnal equinox.

A line drawn directly above the place of birth, intersecting the Ascendant/Descendant axis is the Mid-heaven or M.C. (medium coeli), forming the cusp of the tenth house related to the sign Capricorn and the winter solstice.

The line which is directly opposite the Mid-heaven, again intersecting the Ascendant/Descendant axis, is the I.C. (or Nadir), forming the cusp of the Fourth House, related to the sign Cancer and the summer solstice . The other eight houses fall into the four 'quadrants' determined by these four angles.

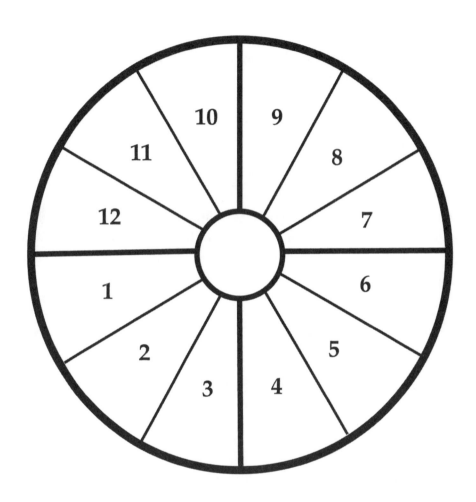

Aspects

As planets are located on the wheel of the Zodiacal circle, aspects are determined by the number of degrees (1-360) between any two planets situated on the wheel. The major aspects indicate either a basic harmonious resonance between the two planets, such as 'sextiles,' (60 degrees apart), and 'trines,' (120 degrees apart); or an 'afflicting' or tense resonance between the two planets, such as 'squares,' (90 degrees), and 'oppositions' (180 degrees apart). Conjunctions are formed by two planets occupying positions close to each other on the wheel. The quality of a conjunction depends upon the nature of the two planets involved.

The symbols and color codes which I use for these basic aspects are as follows:

✳ - sextile - 60 degrees - green

△ - trine - 120 degrees - blue

▢ - square - 90 degrees - orange

☍ - opposition - 189 degrees - red

♂ - conjunction - 0 degrees - purple

Hopefully, the above explanations will serve as a sufficient intro-duction to this symbolic system. Familiarizing oneself with the various symbols and explanations will facilitate your understanding of the Astrological discussions presented in this book.

---

1   This is in contrast to the Eastern or Vedic Astrological system, an explanation of which is beyond the scope of this book.

BIBLIOGRAPHY

Davis, Kenneth C. *Don't Know Much About History: Everything You Need to Know About American History but Never Learned.* Avon Books. 1991.

Hall, Manly P. *America's Assignment With Destiny.* Los Angeles. Philosophical Research Society. 1994.

Heline, Corinne. *America's Invisible Guidance.* Santa Monica, CA. New Age Bible and Philosophy Center. 1994.

Hieronimus, Robert, Ph.D. *America's Secret Destiny: Spiritual Vision & the Founding of a Nation.* Rochester, VT. Destiny Books. 1989.

Hilarion. *Astrology Plus.* Queensville, Ont., Canada. Marcus Books. 1987.

Hilarion. *Nations.* Queensville, Ont., Canada. Marcus Books. 1984.

Hilarion. *More Answers.* Queensville, Ont., Canada. Marcus Books. 1985.

Hilarion. *The Nature of Reality.* Queensville, Ont., Canada. Marcus Books. 1990.

Huber, Bruno & Louise. *The Astrological Houses:A Psychological View of Man & His World.* York Beach, ME. Samuel Weiser. 1984.

Oken, Alan. *Alan Oken's Complete Astrology.* New York. Bantam. 1988.

Omarr, Sydney. *Answer in the Sky.* Charlottesville, VA. Hampton Roads. 1995.

Rudhyar, Dane. *The Astrology of America's Destiny.* New York. Random House. 1974.

Sasportas, Howard. *The Twelve Houses.* Wellingborough, England. Aquarian Press. 1985.

Weatherford, Jack. *Indian Givers: How the Indians of the Americas Transformed the World.* New York. Fawcett Columbine. 1988.

Williamson, Marianne. *The Healing of America.* New York. Simon &Schuster. 1997.

Supplemental to the Second Edition

Andersen, Christopher, *George and Laura: Portrait of an American Marriage,* Harper Collins, New York, NY, 2002

Barber, Benjamin R., *Jihad Vs. McWorld: Terrorism's Challenge to Democracy,* Ballantine Books, New York, NY., 1995.

Brinkley, Douglas, *Tour of Duty,* Harper Collins, New York, NY, 2004

Bruni, Frank, *Ambling into History: The Unlikely Odyssey of George W. Bush,* Harper Collins, New York, NY, 2002

Bush, Barbara, *Barbara Bush: A Memoir,* Charles Scribner's Sons, Lisa Drew Books, 1994.

Bush, George W., *A Charge to Keep: My Journey to the White House,* Harper Collins, New York, NY., 1999

Dean, John W., *Worse Than Watergate: The Secret Presidency of George W. Bush,* Little Brown and Company, New York, NY., 2004

Hatfield, J.H., *Fortunate Son: George W. Bush and The Making of an American President,* Omega Publishing Endeavors, New York, NY, 2000

Kranish, Michael; Mooney, Brian C., ; Easton, Nina J., *John F. Kerry: The Complete Biography By The Boston Globe Reporters Who Know Him Best,* Public Affairs Reports, New York, NY., 2004

Levi, *The Aquarian Gospel of Jesus the Christ,* Devorss.

Minutaglio, Bill, *First Son: George W. Bush and the Bush Family Dynasty,* Three Rivers Press, New York, NY., 1999

Needleman, Jacob, *The American Soul: Rediscovering the Wisdom of the Founders,* Jeremy P. Tarcher/Putnam, New York, NY., 2002

Roy, Arundhati, *War Talk,* South End Press, Cambridge, MA., 2003

Suskind, Ron, *The Price of Loyalty: George W. Bush, The White House, and the Education of Paul O'Neill,* Simon and Schuster, New York, NY, 2004

ACKNOWLEDGMENTS

There are many individuals to whom I am grateful for adding their part to bringing this project to manifestation. I am particularly grateful to my friend and editor Cleve Ives for his diligence and patience with a fledgling writer. I am also very grateful to Maurice Cooke for his work in bringing the words and wisdom of Hilarion to us, and for permission to quote freely from that information. I also want to thank Rob and Laura Enslin for their kind words in the Foreword, Tanya Mann for her material and moral support, Steve Anthes for his work on the cover, Tod Dickey for other computer related support, Elaine and Dan Donley for all their help, Nancy Bennett for photography, and to all my personal friends and clients whose wisdom and insights have added to this work.

THE HILARION SERIES

For those interested in obtaining publications channeled from the Ascended Master Hilarion you may contact the publisher directly at the following address. A complete catalogue is available on request.

Marcus Books
P.O. Box 327
Queensville, Ontario,
Canada, L0G 1R0

ABOUT THE AUTHOR

Steffan Vanel was born in Akron, Ohio on September 25, 1951 at 11:51 AM. He was raised in Massachusetts and Georgia, lived several years in Europe, and currently resides in Washington State.

He is known internationally for his unique synthesis of Astrology, Tarot, Kabballah and Psychology. He is also a primary exponent of the information received from the Master Hilarion.

He travels extensively giving lectures, classes and workshops. His public schedule can be viewed on his website:

www.spiritualcompany.com

Steffan is also available for private Astrology and Tarot consultations, in person or by telephone . Details may be found on his website or by writing the publisher.

ORDER FORM

For additional copies of this book inquire at your local bookstore or send an order to:

Spiritual Company Press
P.O. Box 476
Curlew, WA 99118

Shipping:

U.S./Canada: $4 for the 1st book and $2.00 for each additional.

International: $9 for the 1st book and $5 for each addtional.

Washington State residents:

Please add 8.8% Sales Tax for books shipped to Washington State addresses.